Looking at stars at three in the morning

By Sarah Sprules

Also by Sarah Sprules

Knighton Gorges: The Curse of Thomas Becket

To my wonderful husband, my amazing children and my brilliant Dad and Step-Mum, who are always there with their support, whenever I need it. I love you all very much and wouldn't be who I am, or where I am, without you all xxxxxxxx.

Contents

About This Book

I have read several fiction books where the main character has Autism or Asperger's Syndrome and although they were excellent books and anything that gets people interested in this subject is fantastic, the ones I read seemed to share a similar theme. The main character with a diagnosis was always a boy and the parents (mothers especially) seemed unable to cope with their son and the family unit had broken down as a result. I am in no way, understating how hard it can be as a parent of a child with special needs, but I just know that for me, it isn't all doom and gloom and I wanted to share the joys of having such special children.

Now, everyone knows the old adage, 'write about what you know' and as I am lucky enough to be blessed with two children who have Asperger's Syndrome, I decided to write a book based on three months in my family's life.

My book has two diagnosed characters (one of which is a girl!) I wanted to almost make the Asperger's a secondary thing and I wanted to show in a positive light, how much fun it is to have two little Aspies and after ten years, my husband and I are still happily married.

For us, getting a diagnosis was a positive thing. How can you deal with something, unless you know what it is you're dealing with ? In my experience, everyone I mention Autism or Asperger's to, has brought forth a lot of understanding and compassion. There is far more general awareness of these conditions out there now, so I'm never afraid to talk to anyone about it. I'm taking the 'be loud, be proud' route.

To spare any blushes, I have changed the names to protect the not so innocent and the Santa incident did happen, but not at the children's school. I also had to change a couple of locations and the timing of some events in the name of artistic licence.

I have to say that my children are very lucky to go to a really wonderful school, which is led by a fantastic Head and her team and in my everyday life, I am actually a member of the PTA and am very supportive of the hard work they carry out, on behalf of the children.

As much as possible, I wanted to give an honest snapshot into the lives of a family, with two Aspie kids. My dearest wish is that, people who have children with special needs or are interested in Asperger's Syndrome, Pathological Demand Avoidance or Autistic Spectrum Disorder, might learn a little bit about the condition, without having to read a formal text book. But as the saying goes, 'once you've met one person with Autism, you've met one person with Autism.' It really is a huge spectrum and my children are vastly different from each another, there are however, core elements that remain the same, so some people might not identify with everything in the book, but I hope that they will identify with a lot of it, especially just the way, we pull together as a family to enjoy our life with our special kids.

Chapter One - Girl's Day Out

Grabbing Hope by her warm, chubby little hand, I drew in a deep calming breath and took a trembling step forward into the inky blackness and the terror that awaited us.

My ever dependable husband John, with his blue grey green eyes, that could still make me weak at the knees after ten years of being together had taken our oldest child, Jamie to the local science museum for the afternoon. Whilst, I had the dubious honour of taking our little daughter Hope for her first visit to a cinema.

This was also the first time that Hope and I had been on a mother-daughter day out and she was thoroughly enjoying the fact that she was allowed to go somewhere fun and didn't have to share me (or the sweets) with her Daddy or her brother.

So far, she had already made me divert to her favourite fast food outlet for a burger, chips and a drink, before giving me a list of treats she expected, to watch the film with. I honestly don't know where she puts her food. She eats double what her brother does and she looks so dinky and petite, then all of a sudden you pick her up and realise she's as heavy as an anvil. John has actually had to go and have physiotherapy on his back, because she weighs a ton and he can't say no, when she turns her big blue eyes on him and says "Daddy, I'm tired. Can you carry me ?"

I am the very proud Mummy of two children, Jamie aged nine, who is tall and thin, with honey blonde hair and thick black glasses and Hope who looks like a little princess and is aged four, they are both gorgeous, clever and funny and they also both happen to have Asperger's Syndrome and Pathological Demand Avoidance.

I have a policy of saying 'they have Asperger's.' I never say they are 'Autistic.' It's a small distinction, but to me, it makes all the difference. One means they 'also' have Asperger's the other one means, that they are 'defined' by the Autism and that's not who they are. If you ask Hope what having Asperger's means, she would say "it's what my brother has and I have." If you ask Jamie, he would say it means that they are part of a group of super intelligent people.

There is a saying that goes 'if you've met one person with autism, you've met one person with autism.' It is sooo true. Even my two kids prove this. They both have the exact same diagnosis and yet they are both so different. Jamie is full of anxieties and living with him feels like walking on eggshells all of the time. He has 1-2-1 support at school and has really rubbish motor skills. He is Mensa level intelligent and yet still wets himself, he is a child of opposites. Then we have little Hope, who is feisty, stubborn and needs to be in control at all times. They are both so challenging and charming and if I could give them a pill that would mean they would wake up tomorrow minus the autism, I honestly, hand on heart, don't think I would do it. If you took the Asperger's away, you would take away their personality and all the things that makes them, them. I thank God every day, that they're mine.

Now, I don't like going to see a film at the cinema at the best of times. I would much rather buy a DVD and view it in the warm, comfortable confines of my own living room, than have to sit near a kid who chats incessantly and kicks my seat (incidentally, I'm not referring to my own children here, I actually don't mind them,) but this was Hope's day and Hope's choice and I have to say, her excitement was really quite infectious. With her gigantic ocean blue eyes and long golden hair that even Rapunzel would be jealous of, no one could say "no" to such a little princess.

Loaded down with a veritable bucket of popcorn, fizzy drinks, pink rhinestone studded ear defenders and enough sweets to safely ensure that she didn't come down from her sugar high for the next two months, we found our seats.

Hope couldn't believe that she was in one room that had so many seats in it and I had to tell her to stop looking over the back of her seat, giggling and pointing at annoyed looking people, because it's rude and she's not. To prove me wrong (which is the meaning of her feisty little life) she blew a raspberry at my face. I don't really know why I was surprised. Last night, John laughingly said to her "you are the cause of all our problems" and without even thinking about it, she shot back "and you are the balls of all my problems." I was so shocked, I actually spat my coffee out and John almost fell off the bed. If you ask her what she wants to be when she grows up, she will say

"Darth Vader" and stomps around the house in her dressing gown, humming the Imperial March, whenever she enters or exits a room.

The lights dimmed even further, before extinguishing themselves altogether and Hope threw herself onto my lap in a fit of pure panic, narrowly avoiding spilling my gallon of icy lemonade everywhere.

By the time the adverts and trailers for forthcoming films I had no intention of seeing, had finished, so had our genuinely huge stash of munchies. A lack of popcorn was apparently, an even greater cause for alarm than the darkness had been and Hope decided to herself, that she would simply go and get some more from the friendly woman in the cinema lobby, as quickly as possible, so she didn't miss any more of the film than she had to. I barely had time to grab my purse, and was forced into leaving our coats and my handbag behind, as I sprinted behind her with an acceleration that even Usain Bolt would be proud of, (whilst crouched over, so I wasn't obstructing everyone else's view of the film. Which made my speed even more impressive.)

When I finally caught up with her, I tried to talk to her about not running off, but she was far too giddy with the excitement of the cinema (and too high with sugar) to listen and I really didn't want to ruin her special day by chastising her too harshly, so I grabbed her hand and we rushed to spend more money on yet more sugary goods.

We returned to our seats with yet another mountain of sweetened popped corn and I was endlessly thankful to find that no one had decided to steal my bag, which contained the usual, pink blinged up ear defenders, a spare pair of pants and socks (for Hope, not me) and a large radar key, for emergency access to disable toilets. No expensive compact or designer sunglasses for me, no, I carry pants and a radar key, that's how I roll!

The sound was blasting out of the speakers, but she didn't seem to mind and I looked at her little head, as she in her seat and thought how proud I was of my big girl. Unfortunately, in the very same minute that she had forced the last fistful of popcorn into her little mouth, Hope suddenly remembered that she was wearing shoes with exceedingly bright red lights on (kind of like having an annoying laser pen in your eye, whenever you looked in her direction.)

As if she had never seen them before, she sprang out of her seat and started dancing around, laughing hysterically at how her shoes sparkled in the dimness of the cinema. Finally, I managed to settle my twirling princess down and breathed a huge sigh of relief, causing the woman in front of me to turn around and glare in disgust (I've never felt more like blowing a raspberry at someone in my whole life. Damn it that must be where Hope gets it from.)

An amusing bit of slapstick violence, will always grab Hope's attention and she sat laughing loudly at the movie once more. I could actually feel my muscles beginning to slowly unwind, when she announced in an extremely loud voice (perfectly timed with a pause in the film dialogue, I might add.) "Mummy, Poo's trying to come out of my bum."

Luckily my blushes weren't so obvious in the gloomy cinema, so I grabbed her hot little hand and rushed her back down to the toilets, as fast as I possibly could, with Hope laughing and chattering beside me all the way there. After several minutes of sitting there, grinning at me, she triumphantly declared, in a conspiratorial whisper. "I don't really need to go to the toilet."

I think we had been sat back in our seats for all of five minutes, when she whispered "Mummy, I need to go wee wee." Now, I'm not sure if it was the way she giggled as she ran down the ramp towards the double doors, or it was the way that she sat laughing on the toilet and failing to produce the goods, that I finally realised, I was being played, by a master of manipulation and I didn't even see it, until now. Hope knows that whenever she plays the toilet card, I am powerless to defy her and she was ready to play. As we walked back through the lobby, the woman who overheard me say "I'm not taking you to the toilet again for the rest of the film, so don't even try it," must have thought I was one heartless bitch.

We finally made it through to the end of the seemingly endless film, without further distraction techniques being deployed. As we walked out through the double glass doors into the bright sunlight outside, Hope looked at me and without any trace of irony in her innocent blue eyes, said "I can't wait to go to the cinema again. I was a good girl to sit down and watch the film wasn't I ?" I smiled and nodded at her expectant face, because I thought that otherwise there was a distinct possibility that I might have actually started weeping, right then and there in the middle of the car park.

As we drove back towards home, a news report came on the radio that said parents of disabled children have the highest divorce rates, but parents of children with Asperger's Syndrome have the highest divorce rates of all families coping with a disability. I promptly flicked on the CD player and Katy Perry played through the speakers, singing a reassuringly upbeat song about birthdays. I was far too tired to hear depressing news right now. A bit of Katy Perry was just what I needed. Taking Hope to the cinema felt like I had just gone ten rounds with a heavyweight and lost.

Driving along the familiar roads, my mind started to wander and I realised that I desperately needed to do something for myself. I used to have a job in a nursery, but in the very same week that I qualified as a Nursery Nurse (after studying really hard for months) I unfortunately got made redundant. This was coincidentally, the same week that Hope was diagnosed with Asperger's Syndrome (and the mythical and much sought after diagnosis of Pathological Demand Avoidance.)

I suddenly found myself being a stay at home carer and I actually loved it, but I soon found out, that my life had no room in it for anything that wasn't kid related and I didn't have much to talk about, when I did mix with adults.

We already have a son with exactly the same diagnosis, so it wasn't a shock at all, in fact it was more of a relief when Hope got diagnosed. I don't really see the point of being reluctant to have a label or wanting to remain in denial about it (but I know that makes me different to a lot of others and I can completely understand that.) At least with a name to put on it, you get much more understanding from others, you know what you're dealing with and also it meant that there was a reason that Hope seemed to be a hormonal little minx and we were all relieved about that.

As much as I loved spending time with my beautiful little girl (I missed her on the few mornings when she was at nursery,) carrying out her litany of demands is quite a time consuming job. Being Hope's Mummy is something akin to being the only servant of an organised and ruthless dictator, (I should imagine.)

During my rare, carer free moments, I took the opportunity to go along to as many Autism courses as I could possibly find. My plan being, that when I finally did return to work, I could work alongside children who are on the Autistic Spectrum. I still have my qualifications to lean on, for when Hope takes the next scary step of going to school.

All of this was great and good for my career prospects as well as for my children, but I realised that I need some sort of creative outlet, something that was mine alone, some sort of hobby. All of my time is spent with the children (which don't get me wrong, I absolutely love and I wouldn't have it any other way. (I didn't want to recapture my lost youth by going out clubbing.) Yet, I realised that I wanted something to talk to John about, when he comes home from work, that doesn't revolve around kid's programmes or what the playground gossip was. I needed to take a step outside of my comfort zone. (I hate that phrase. It's right up there with 'touch base' and 'state of play' but nevertheless, it was what I needed.) I would have to have a serious think about what I really wanted to do. Maybe lion taming or juggling, something different. I don't think I've got the patience for watercolour painting.

Chapter Two - City Escape

Sometimes as a parent, we plan things that we think our kids would like, based on what we ourselves actually would have liked when we were children. Often these two things don't always amount to the same thing. This was blatantly apparent, the day we sat the kids down a couple of months ago and told them the exciting news (well, we thought it was exciting,) that we wanted to take them away for a long weekend to a lovely caravan park in Cornwall. We chose the particular site carefully, because it was near the sea, had a kids club with entertainment and an amusement arcade. It looked perfect.

The plan was to take advantage of Jamie having an inset day and escape to the coast and have fun. We thought that, as every day is so difficult and draining for the kids, they deserved a little break. We thought they'd be thrilled... We were wrong!

Between them, they listed the reasons in detail, that they hated our carefully thought out idea. Apparently travelling the three hour drive to Cornwall, is too long to be in the car. They don't like the beach and Jamie hates the sea (news to us), the kids club is boring, the entertainment is too loud and the amusements contain terrifying games that have zombies and mummies in them and (in Jamie's opinion) should be banned.

Faced with their joint, abject disappointment, we asked them what they would rather do… So, we ended up booking a stay in a budget hotel in sunny Manchester! Yes that's right, we gave our kids the option of going anywhere on a mini break and they chose Manchester. (Which incidentally, takes two hours longer to get to, than Cornwall, which was apparently too far to go!)

For Jamie's birthday last year, he had asked us to take him to Manchester for our first visit to the city, all because he wanted to visit the Legoland Discovery Centre. Despite the five hour car journey, they had loved it and they had found something they liked even more than Legoland itself, (shopping in the Trafford Centre.)

So it was that we found ourselves at the end of yet another five hour journey, staying for two nights this time (at the children's insistence.) We had somehow managed to arrive an hour before check in and the kids were really grumpy and bored, so we pulled up outside the hotel and I sprinted into reception, leaving a very harassed looking John in the car with the two terrors.

"Hi. I know we're early" I said, flashing my brightest smile at the surly woman behind the desk. "My children are quite stressed out after a long journey and I wondered if our room was ready ? I appreciate that it's a little early." She didn't miss a beat, staring at me over the gold rims of her round glasses, as she sneered. "No, it's too early. There are no rooms ready for occupation, until the two o'clock check in time." I totally understand that they might not actually have had any rooms available and there is a check in time for a reason, but her blatantly unhelpful attitude had begun to annoy me. She didn't even trouble herself to check if what she was saying was right. "Oh OK" I said pleasantly "I just thought that because the kids were playing up, it was worth asking anyway." Regarding me, like a lioness deciding whether she could be bothered to throw out a lazy paw and crush her prey, she just said "sorry" in a tone that pretty much suggested the opposite. It was then, that I decided to have one last roll of the dice and shamelessly played my trump card, as I began to walk away. I said. "It's just that they have Autism you see." What do you know, my words hit the target!

Once again, she didn't even blink, didn't have to consult a computer screen or pick up a phone to check a change in status, she just said, without any shame or apology for her previously cold manner. "No problem at all. I can let you have room 1201. How many keys would you like ?"

Grumpy after such a long journey and trying not to feel a little disgruntled at the receptionist, I decided to concentrate on the children and not ruin the atmosphere.

I have genuinely, never seen the kids so excited to get into a hotel room before and within two minutes we had to start shushing them. This particular hotel chain has a guarantee policy for a good night's sleep and we were terrified of being thrown out and forced to drive all the way home again. (The chances of which were fairly high, Hope sounds like a herd of elephants by herself, so when you factor in Jamie, who has to run around everywhere instead of walking, it wouldn't take long for them to get us kicked out, if left unchecked.)

After fifteen minutes of being in our room, everything in the suitcases had been unpacked, a kids TV channel was on, showing an animated show that the kids usually liked and I had literally just put my lips to the mug, happily anticipating my first sip of lovely hot coffee, when the "I'm bored" loop started in the corner from Jamie. I must have been about half the way through my coffee, before I finally reacted. I had tried to be strong and not give him an audience, but I just couldn't withstand the verbal onslaught any longer. Less than five minutes later, we stepped out of the hotel's tiny lift and headed out to their favourite place in the whole world, the Trafford Centre, for a 'quick look around.'

When they were younger, we tried to get them interested in walking around the woods, but it soon became apparent that our kids were never going to be the outdoorsy type and their greatest passion is looking around shops. We have got a big mall about twenty minutes from our house and people come from all over to visit it. I think our mall could fit into the Trafford Centre about three times. The whole food court there, is about the same size as our whole mall. The kids like to sit in the ship themed restaurant area and there's a huge choice of food variety, which is good for other kids, but not mine. They don't like too many options. In fact, if we stayed in Manchester for a week, they would still want pizza every day. I must say, in defence of their materialistic pursuits, they don't actually spend that much money or whine until they get whatever they want. They have their pocket money and they always stick to their budget. Also, because the shopping centres are flat, they tend to walk farther than they would anywhere else, because they don't get so tired.

A mere six hours later, laden with several shopping bags and stomachs filled with copious amounts of pizza and ice cream, we all returned to the hotel room, exhausted and happy.

As we lay cuddled up in bed, under the crisp white duvet, drinking our hot chocolates, I looked at the kids and felt so happy that they we were, having some much needed family time together. John works six days a week and we don't get to spend as much time as we would like, together as a family.

Putting my chocolate down, I reached out and gave both the kids a hug, immediately getting swatted away, as if I were an annoying mosquito… So much, for loving family moments. I really should know better by now.

Chapter Three - Kiss Me Quick

In the early hours of a cold Manchester morning, we were woken up earlier than on a school day (what's that about ? Normally I can't get them out of bed in the mornings.)

In the darkness provided by the thick, blackout curtains, I could just make out two human shapes, slowly advancing on me, like something out of a horror film. Before I could call to John for help. I was leapt on, by two manic children. "Come on, get up. We want food." They giggled, as they bounced up and down on the stomach, that had been ruined in the process of carrying and giving birth to these two mercenaries and was now in complete agony.

Always the last to know what's going on, John leapt up in panic and then sank back down with a groan as he realised what was happening. This was enough for the kids to switch their focus onto their next target and I was left reeling in agony, as they pounced on their poor father.

Once we were up and dressed, the kids marched us down to a very expensive, all you can eat buffet breakfast. Jamie (who normally goes out of his way to try and not eat) took one bite of virtually everything on offer and probably spent a total of five minutes with his posterior touching the seat, out of the whole twenty minutes that we were actually there for. His side of the table was adorned with plates of nibbled items and four bowls that were virtually filled to their brims with uneaten cereal. To say nothing of the array of half-drunk juices of various varieties, that were piled up at the side. The thing is, another parent might have scolded him for all that he had wasted, but I was just thrilled by what he actually had eaten. Because he had little bits, of a lot of different things, he'd been tricked into eating more than he usually would and I was ecstatic, even though the waitress was sending us withering looks and huffing every time she had to come and clean our table.

Yesterday, we had spent all day doing what the children wanted (and already most of this morning.) Today was going to be my day (John's obviously not allowed to have a day, his reward is in us allowing him to come along on whatever we want to do.)

Today we were heading to the iconic 'Las Vegas of the North,' Blackpool. I don't really think that Jamie, John or Hope were looking forward to it all that much, but as I told them, it was an experience, that they wouldn't forget. Following the trip, they would always be able to say that they had been to Blackpool. To be honest (and the bit that I didn't tell them beforehand) this part of the trip was actually, non-negotiable.

Jamie and Hope get to veto just about every suggestion that John and I make, well not this time. We were going to Blackpool no matter what! (Why did I want to go to Blackpool so much ?) Well, as luck would have it, Madame Tussauds at Blackpool, just happened to have Katy Perry's wax figure visiting for a few weeks and I was determined to see it.

I probably haven't mentioned this before, but I have a serious Katy Perry obsession. I could give both my kids a run for their money in the obsessions department, when it comes to that particular raven haired songbird. She is the reason that I did something very naughty for myself, a few months ago. Ever since I've had the kids, every single penny that I've spent, has been on them. I even cut my own fringe, so I don't have to pay money, going to the hairdressers. I buy my clothes from the supermarket, so that they can walk around in designer clobber.) That all changed, the day that Miss Perry confirmed that she was embarking on a worldwide tour, that would kick off in the UK. The morning that the tickets went on sale, I made John take the kids to school and nursery, whilst I sat with a mobile phone in one hand, a landline phone in the other, a PC to my left and a laptop (well in my lap, obviously.) I was a woman on a mission. I didn't even want to consider the fact that I might not get a ticket. I wanted this more, than Charlie Bucket wanted a golden ticket.

I was beginning to hyperventilate, when I managed to find two tickets (one for me and one for my friend who I was treating, because John had to stay at home and look after the kids.) The price for both tickets, came up on the screen as £360 (I had offered to get Hope a ticket, but she had refused, because of the people and the noise.) I could see the time ticking down on the internet and I rang John immediately. I squealed down the phone at him in excitement. "I've found two tickets, amazing seats and they're £360 for the two, so is it OK if I book them?" John sort of did a weird, irritated snort and then said the words that I really didn't want to hear, when I had only one minute eighteen seconds left to complete my purchase. "No way, we're not paying that." The tickets were in my grasp and I was going to be at that concert, come hell or high water. So my response was, "I HAVE to go." John thought that meant, I had to end the call, because I was so upset. So he said "OK then" meaning, 'sorry, you can't go, I understand you don't want to talk about it now, so I'll say goodbye for now.' But I took it as 'OK then, I accept that you have to book these tickets, as it's the most important event in your life, since you had the kids' and I slammed my finger down on the button to buy those two bad boys, before someone else stole, what was rightfully mine.

When John came home and apologised that I couldn't go and I told him excitedly, that I had two fantastic seats, he didn't speak to me for at least three hours. He was madder than he had ever been with me in ten years of being together. As for me, I was completely unrepentant. I was going to see Katy Perry.

Madame Tussauds is an interesting place to visit anyway, but even more so with two Aspie children. Hope was totally overwhelmed by it all and was really scared of the lifelike mounds of wax and hid behind my legs at every opportunity. Jamie ran around taking selfies with every single figure in the place, even if he didn't always know who they were, whilst John and I just walked around taking it all in and admiring the celebrity likenesses (or laughing at the really bad ones) and generally saying "well I never knew he was so tall," or "she was so thin," over and over again.

I entered one of the last rooms and saw Katy Perry there on the stage (wax one obviously, not the real Katy Perry.) The room dissolved, so that all I could see was her and I'm sure I heard angel's singing. I'm not embarrassed (though I probably should be) to say, that I dropped my handbag on the floor as soon as I saw her and ran full pelt at my idol. John took LOTS of photos of her and I together and then gently suggested that I should move away from the waxwork, whilst Jamie rolled his eyes at me and Hope looked panic stricken as she didn't know where she could hide, now that I was betraying her with one of the scary figures. I honestly think, if I had thought it at all possible, I would have picked her up (Katy Perry, not Hope) and run right out of the building with my precious one. Reluctantly, I took a last look and followed the others out of the room. I had seen what I wanted to see and at least I had photos to prove it. Feeling such excitement at a wax image, I dread to think what I would be like if I actually met Katy Perry in real life. Can't wait for the concert, not long now!

After the obligatory fish and chips on a blustery Blackpool seafront (Hope and Jamie flatly refused to go up the famous tower,) there didn't seem much else to do, so we headed back to Manchester and the kids beloved Trafford Centre (and more pizza,) before spending our last night in our cosy little hotel room.

Chapter Four - Putting Me In My Place

Driving home after our successful weekend, the kids were happily sat in the back of the car with their headphones on, watching one of their many animated DVDs. Taking advantage of a momentary lapse in the chaos that is our lives. John's head was resting against the window, as he dozed, tired from the weekend's full on activities and I was left to my own thoughts. (A very rare time indeed.)

I often find that my thoughts usually get interrupted, or I can't hear my own inner monologue and can't make a decision on anything, because the kid's chatter is relentless and I honestly can't think straight. I've lost count of the times that I've walked out of a shop because I just couldn't decide what to buy, because of their endless prattle. So a couple of hours of peace was amazing. I always say, "You know you're a mum, when having an uninterrupted bath is an achievement and not a regular occurrence."

So much downtime, gave my mind time to wander and I desperately tried to decide what I wanted to do for a hobby. I'd already discounted night school (don't want to be away from the kids for too long on a weekly basis.) I'm not really the stamp collecting sort and I would have gone to an amateur dramatics group, but I'm intimidated by the audition process (sort of like the X Factor, but in a church hall and twice the amount of people judging you. Or at least that was what I told myself.) When I kept coming up empty for ideas, I finally decided that the best course of action would be, to have a look at local community centres and clubs to see what's about. There might be more in the whole of my city, than is dreamt of in my little philosophy.

We arrived home safe, but exhausted (even John who had spent most of the journey asleep.) The car was filled with all of the kids purchases (of which there were many, due to there being loads of shops in Manchester, that we don't have at home) and although we had only been away for two nights, we had packed so much fun into such a short time, it felt like we had been gone for a whole week and the pile of dirty laundry certainly amounted to a week's worth.

After unpacking and putting the washing machine on for the first of several loads, we sat, talking over a coffee about how much we wanted to move house. "When we move nearer to your school" I said to Jamie, "you'll be able to go and call for your friends and go out to play with them." Now, I thought that this was a nice suggestion, but clearly I had forgotten who I was talking to. "Are you mad, woman ?" He asked. "Have you never heard of paedophiles ? Do you want me to get murdered ?" As he stormed up to his bedroom, clearly disgusted at my lack of parenting skills, he said "I won't be calling for any friends until I'm eighteen years old, thank you."

It's such a horrible feeling, when you realise how disappointed in you, your child is. He questions everything I say and really doesn't trust me (because he knows best) so I'm starting to think that he's never going to believe me capable of raising children. Especially, when he thinks I clearly have a flagrant disregard for their safety. You'd have thought that I'd just stood at the side of the road asking motorists to offer him sweets.

The last time that he had been so disparaging of me as a mother, was when I had left him and Hope in the house to go and get them an ice cream from the ice cream van, which was literally parked across the road from our gate. It took me all of six steps to get there from our front garden. (I know this because I actually went back later and counted.) When I went to push the front door open, I saw it was locked. Letting myself in with their two cones, I saw that the curtains had been drawn in the middle of the day. I walked in, thinking that perhaps the sun had been shining on the TV and that was why everything was now in darkness. Peering into the gloom, I handed them their ice creams and said "what's with the curtains ?" Jamie was livid with indignation, he had one hand planted firmly on his hip and brandishing an ice cream in my direction with the other. He glared accusingly. "Do you know how irresponsible you are ? Wait until Daddy gets home and I tell him what you did. You left us in the house alone and I had to close the curtains in case the police were outside and found out. You could actually go to prison for this."

Trying not to laugh, I bit my lip, apologised and promised never to do it again. There really was no point in arguing with him. I don't think he realised that the downside of this was that I would never get him an ice cream from the van ever again. Lesson learned.

Chapter Five - I'm With A Skater Boy

Jamie had been invited to a birthday party. It should be a good thing, whenever he gets invited anywhere, but honestly it's really a Catch 22 situation. I find it so heart breaking, when he doesn't get invited to one and you see his hopeful little face, as the birthday brat (sorry, I mean boy or girl) hands out the invitations to everyone except him.

I know that a lot of children who are like him and have Asperger's, Autism or are different in any way, might never get invited to parties at all. (Sadly I speak from experience, after talking to mums on the Autism courses,) so I do try and remind myself that I should really feel very grateful, when he is one of the chosen few.

The only problem is, the games. Jamie usually has a breakdown when he doesn't win at pass the parcel for example and he lacks the motor skills for things like musical statues, because he can't balance and he can't stay still for more than a couple of seconds, even if his life depended on it.

A usual party will consist of me, trying to prepare him for about an hour beforehand and him insisting that if he doesn't win, he'll be fine and then, he loses at something and instantly has a meltdown in the middle of the floor and we have to leave halfway through, with me giving lots of apologies, but failing to get any cake.

The particular party he was about to go to was a roller skating one, which is yet another source of angst and I would have bet money on the fact that I would be back home within an hour of the start, with my son weeping noisily into his pillow and refusing to go to any more 'stupid parties.' (I realise that this seems quite a specific scenario, but I've been through this several times already.)

The last time that Jamie put on a pair of skates, was when he was four years old. He was happily skating around the living room and I ran to the back door to let the dog out, who was crossing his legs in his desire not to have an accident all over my wooden flooring. As I closed the door behind the VERY relieved pooch, I heard a loud bang. Running back into the living room, I found Jamie sitting in the grate with a really shocked expression on his face.

Picking him up. I just had enough time to ask him what had happened, when he went totally limp like a rag doll. I had been balancing Jamie on my hip, when he fell backwards and the back of his head hit my knee. He was as grey as John Major's Spitting Image puppet and I was more scared than I ever have been in my life. I began screaming and trying to wake him up, all my composure and first aid training flying right out the window. In my panicked state, I rang for an ambulance immediately, but by the time the medics actually arrived (which was probably about eight minutes later, but easily felt like four hours) my little boy was running around as if nothing had happened.

(Literally running around with a flashing torch and chattering away, about his skates.) He explained that he had fallen and caught his spine on the grate, which had then shocked him and made him faint and he was certain that he hadn't hit his head at all (Huge Relief! Quite useful on that occasion, to have a child who is so articulate too.)

We were taken to the local children's hospital in an ambulance, which was very exciting for a four year old and he proceeded to give the paramedics a guided tour of the sights that we passed en route to the children's hospital. John met us there, looking terrified by the whole event (at this point Hope wasn't born yet) and we were left in a room for an hour and a half before Jamie was given a blue balloon on a stick and discharged, with a piece of paper for signs of concussion, on the off chance that he had bumped his head and just couldn't remember. As soon as we got home, I threw away the darned skates that had hurt my beloved son and caused us all such a scare.

So understandably, I was terrified at the prospect of Jamie being on eight wheels again (he's clumsy enough when he's wearing normal shoes on a flat surface, let alone ones with wheels fixed to them.) He has all the coordination of a newly born giraffe on ice (and I am not over-exaggerating.)

As we got there, we walked into the hall, where pop music was blaring out, loud enough to ensure that the children would all be suffering from tinnitus by tomorrow and it was an achievement in itself, that he would even consider being in the same room as all that noise.

He was so slow and he kept falling over, but he didn't give up and inexplicably, he kept going. (Heaven only knows where he found the inner strength from, because he never had it before.) After he had fallen over for the fifth time (and by falling over, I mean, slamming into the floor with his knees and nearly breaking his weak little wrists, as he tried to stop himself.) I went to scoop him up from the middle of the floor, in front of all the other children and he held onto me crying big teardrops onto his little red cheeks. "Come on honey" I soothed "let's go home. It's OK. You don't have to put yourself through this." To my astonishment, he refused. I thought he'd jump at the chance of an excuse to leave, but for once, he was determined. "I'm staying."

The marshals announced that there would be a game of bulldog and my stomach did a somersault in worry. The other kids had all made it to the other side, before Jamie had even reached the middle, yet he kept on going. I walked with him, waiting to catch him if he fell and I kept feeling hot as I saw the other children all waiting for him to finish, so I can't even think how he must have felt. When they couldn't wait any longer, the marshals would shout "bulldog" and without even making it to the other side, Jamie would have to turn around and start all over again. I didn't know he possessed such strength reserves and I don't think I've ever been more proud of him.

As I walked beside my son, a huge lump of raw emotion filled my throat. It occurred to me that this bit of the party was an analogy of Jamie's life. The other kids might be stood watching him, waiting for him, simply getting from A to B might be harder for him than it is for them, but in the end, no matter how hard it was to keep going, or how many times he fell and hurt himself, he got right back up and struggled on. I can't remember ever feeling so positive about his future. In the end, it turned out to be the most challenging party he'd ever been to and yet the most fulfilling too. It taught me never to underestimate my little man.

Chapter Six - Managed Mischief

Today was the day the kids had waited months for. We were going to the Harry Potter Studio Tour near London. This was another occasion, when the kids didn't mind going on a long drive. Funnily enough, the long drive time wasn't even an issue.

We got there, just as the main doors were opened and the kid's excitement was totally infectious. They were both dressed in Harry Potter costumes, but because Jamie already wears black glasses on a daily basis, he really did look like Harry and Hope looked like a mini version of Hermione (I made the unfortunate mistake of telling her this and felt the full might of her wrath, when she assured me in no uncertain terms that she was Harry and NOT Hermione.)

Everything was fine, until we got to the queue, waiting to enter. Jamie had heard from one of his friends at school that the first section you go into is a cinema, but his helpful friend apparently wouldn't tell him what the short movie was about, because she didn't want to ruin the surprise for him. Jamie scoured the internet in vain, but couldn't find any enlightenment, so he started to freak out, as he does when he's faced with the unknown and the unknown was particularly scary this time, given that it was going to happen in the dark.

Trying to keep him calm, we went to the customer services desk and explained our plight to a lady called Janine behind the desk. As soon as I explained that they both have Asperger's, Janine came out from behind her desk and took Jamie to show him a map of the building and tried to allay his fears about the film. By this point, my poor anxious little wizard had passed an invisible line and was now beyond all reasoning and the helpful Janine asked us to wait for a second.

We stood there feeling a little unnerved as she talked into a walkie talkie and the crowds turned to stare in our direction, wondering if we were about to be arrested for some Potter related misdemeanour (like shouting that we preferred Slytherin to Gryffindor, or accidentally showing that we all had tattoos of the dark mark.)

Luckily, we weren't left standing there for long, before Janine asked us to follow her and we were promptly whisked through the back ways that only staff normally see. She allowed us to bypass the cinema altogether and brought us out at the very doors to the great hall. As she left us, we thanked her profusely for her help and for taking the time out to talk to Jamie and show him where he was and where we were going.

Because of a little understanding and kindness, we were able to enjoy our day and the kids definitely made the most of it. When we got to the shop at the very end of the tour. I said to them. "You both have forty pounds each to spend." Personally, I thought that was more than generous. When I was Jamie's age, I would have been grateful (and lucky) to get a pencil or an eraser from the shop, after a day out. My son is a boy of his generation however and his response was "Forty pound's not going to go far is it ? I won't be able to buy much with that." I tried not to be annoyed at him, he is after all, a logical child and was only really speaking the truth. I was determined to stand my ground this time though. "Well tough luck" I whispered under my breath, whilst simultaneously smiling reassuringly at passers-by. "That's all you're getting. Eighty pounds between the two of you is more than enough!"

It felt good, to set boundaries and have the kids respect them. If I stood up to them now, it would save hundreds of pounds in expected toys over the next few years. This was the beginning of a new era.

We went in the shop and came away, having spent one hundred and twenty seven pounds!!!!

As we walked back out through the main entrance doors and the kids were proudly carrying their full bags of merchandise, I was silently hating myself as John alternately glared at me and looked around for my backbone. Jamie turned to me and said, "Mummy can you book more tickets, so that we can come back for Christmas please ?"

Chapter Seven - Little Boy Lost

Jamie came out of school today and I could immediately see from his flushed cheeks that something was very wrong. "Are you OK ?" I asked with concern, wondering what on earth could have happened. Where Jamie's concerned, it could literally be anything from hitting someone, to wetting himself. "Well" he began, in indignation, as I braced myself for an epic tale. "We had a supply teacher today and he told me to pull my socks up."

"Right" I said uneasily, starting to see where this conversation was going. "What happened ?"

"I bent down, pulled my socks up and then showed him, to prove that I'd done what he'd asked." I tried to hold it in, but a groan escaped, as I imagined the children laughing at Jamie's cheekiness and a teacher, stood at the front of the class, with steam coming out of his ears. "What happened then ?"

"I think he was going to tell me off, but my assistant went over and whispered something to him and he just told me that I'd done a good job. If I'd done a good job, why did he look like he was cross and why were they whispering ? I don't like it when people whisper."

Trying to hide my smile, I put my arm around him and as we walked through the playground together. I tried to explain to him, how sometimes people can say one thing, but mean another. I think I managed it sensitively, so he wouldn't feel too embarrassed, but he still looked a bit confused.

Whilst they had been at school and nursery, I had spent two whole hours of house cleaning and as we walked through the front door, the words "keep it tidy" had only just left my lips, when Jamie decided that he wanted to find one of his little toy figures (and by little, I mean two inches high.) Getting angrier and angrier as he went, he proceeded to go through the whole living room, throwing around my perfectly arranged cushions and chairs like a one kid tornado.

Following behind and screaming (not the best way of dealing with a meltdown I know, but hey I'm not perfect and us parents sometimes have meltdowns too.) I finally managed to get him to stop, just as he was about to tip a bucket of Lego over the living room floor. "Jamie" I said, trying to get his attention. "When did you last see your figure ?" He was almost beyond the point of listening to me by now, his eyes were wild and his arms were flailing madly. "It was yesterday." I was pretty sure he had just been playing with it in the car and thought he'd brought it in with him, so despite the fact that he was on the edge, I decided to press further. As he tried to get around me to start moving the sofa (I'm not sure why he thought he could do this, he had a hard enough time, lifting the cushions.) I tackled him. "Didn't you just have your figure ? I'm sure I just saw you playing with it."
"YES! I just put it down there and now it's missing."
He seemed quite indignant, for someone who had only

seconds ago, insisted that he hadn't seen it for a day. "Why did you say you last saw it yesterday then ?" "I don't know, I must have forgot." He screamed, as if he were talking to a moron. Whilst resisting the urge to punch myself violently in the head until I lost consciousness, so that I wouldn't have to continue this utterly insane conversation anymore, I had foolishly managed to hesitate for a mere second and sensing my weakness, Jamie started trashing the room again. I commenced with my screaming again, whilst John and Hope were on their knees checking under the sofas (and trying their best to stay out of the line of verbal fire.) Suddenly, Jamie stood up and said "oh wait, it was in my onesie pocket all along." Sometimes, you really just have to laugh in the face of such craziness, because otherwise it would drive you mad.

Less than an hour later, Jamie was eating a toffee, when I heard him make a weird squeaking sound. I looked up, just as he pulled the toffee out of his mouth, with one of his milk teeth embedded in the sticky, gooey mess and blood pouring from the empty socket. It was all the more shocking for the fact that it hadn't even been wobbling or causing him pain (trust me, when Jamie's in pain, everyone knows about it,) but he was rather more excited about the prospect of tooth fairy money than the tooth itself.

Eagerly, Jamie ran up to his bedroom and placed the bloodied tooth beneath his white pillow. Knowing what a terrible memory I have, I told John to remind the tooth fairy later, that she needed to put the money under Jamie's pillow and to make sure the pillow went on a ninety degree wash, the next day. The tooth fairy has always come through for him and she wasn't going to let him down this time either, despite having a knack for being really forgetful, especially at night, when she's really tired. Getting John to remind 'her' was a win, win situation. Either he would remember, or he would forget and then the 'tooth fairy' would take great satisfaction in berating him for forgetting.

Chapter Eight - Tooth Fairy Tales

At six thirty in the morning, I was rudely awaken by a distraught Jamie, standing in front of me, wearing nothing but his boxer shorts and holding a tooth in his outstretched hand. "Why didn't the tooth fairy come ?" He asked, through his tears. Sometimes I amaze myself, at my ability to swing into action, the second that I wake up.

Leaping out of bed, I told him to go back one more time to check and grabbed a pound out of my purse. Clenching my fist with the coin safely hidden from view, I ran in behind him and told him to stand back. I pretended to put my hand down underneath his bed in the far corner and produced the coin. Jamie was instantly happy and wiped his tears away, but as was usual, he started to immediately over think it, with his amazing ability at over complicating every situation. "Why did she leave the tooth though ?" He sniffled.

Thinking on my feet (without even having drunk my morning cup of coffee,) I mulled it over for a couple of seconds and said "Well you and Hope are up and down throughout the night. I kept waking up and going to the toilet and Daddy got up for work at four this morning. One of us must have disturbed her, she probably dropped the money in a panic and escaped without the tooth. Thankfully, Jamie clearly believed my story and I wondered at my ability to lie so quickly, elaborately and convincingly, when my brain is so tired and befuddled through lack of sleep. John wouldn't be so happy when he got home and I told him off for not reminding the 'tooth fairy' about the money.

With one crisis averted, I was forced to drive straight into another. Parking the car, I dragged two very reluctant children to the Eye Hospital for yet another of Jamie's routine appointments.

Every two months we are forced to sit in a bare waiting room, looking at fish for at least half an hour past our appointment time and then my poor Jamie is subjected to a battery of various sight tests.

When he is in the waiting room, Jamie is my usual, dear sweet boy, but when he is called into that little cubicle, he seems to go through an extraordinary transformation and suddenly becomes 'Autism Boy.'

I even had to change who he sees, because the last lady he was under, was so rude to him. I kept explaining each time, that he had Asperger's Syndrome and her reply was always "well that explains it." Yet each time we went back, she would claim that she knew nothing about his diagnosis. One day she asked him to look at the other end of the room and say what the colour was on the screen, when Jamie answered "black," she said "yes like your future if you don't sit still."

Needless to say, that was the last time he saw her. Being a mum of Aspie kids, you have to be prepared to stick up for your kids, because if they can't, who else is going to do it ?

He's under a lovely girl called Sophia now. She's sweet and positive with blonde hair and more importantly, she is the only member of staff, who hasn't tried to push me into agreeing for Jamie to have an operation. I tell them all, in no uncertain terms that he is not going to be operated on and yet they go behind my back and make referrals for him to see a doctor, which I then have to cancel after first spending days of calming Jamie down.

This morning, Sophia was as wonderful and kind as usual and Jamie managed to keep control of his limbs for ten minutes and the appointment went very well. Jamie also particularly likes the fact that he regularly gets to miss time out of school, so when I dropped him off before lunchtime, he ran in through the school gates quite happily.

I only had a couple of hours at home before I found myself standing in the playground once again, ready to collect him.

For fifteen minutes before school starts in the morning and ends in the afternoon, the playground is a minefield of cliques of women. (There are of course dads there too, but they don't seem to form close little gangs like the women do.) Luckily one of the 'cool' mums seems to like me and so the others tolerate me when they have to. I have a couple of friends who I actually like and they are definitely not part of the 'in crowd' either and that's just the way they like it.

Unfortunately though, none of my friends happened to be here today, they were probably running late and I cursed silently when I saw the worst of the 'popular mums' walking towards me.

Her name is Claudia Greenacre and she is a powerhouse of elitism and snobbery. Her interests are the WI, the PTA, baking, sewing and exercising at the gym, whilst her passion is her full time job as an HR manager. Sadly, her children aren't even on her list of interests or passions. She stands in the playground, a paragon of virtue, swathed in designer clothes, passing on tips of how to bake a perfect Victoria sponge, whilst her son Billy runs around in the same polo shirt he's been wearing for three days at a time (with toothpaste smeared all over the front) and shivers without a sweatshirt or coat in the autumn, bullying the other children because he's so unhappy and starved of affection.

Claudia swaggered over to where I stood, her ponytail bouncing behind her, perfect coiffure as usual. In her linen trousers and soft leather shoes, she looked like a poster girl for a designer outlet, or someone ready to go shooting grouse in the woods, with a Labrador. In comparison, my scuffed ballerina shoes, leggings and chiffon tea dress, teamed with my dark brown dyed hair and carefully applied, yet colourful make up, made me feel like a common streetwalker, when compared next to her. Claudia regaled me with stories of her latest foray into damson jam and the trouble with maintaining the heat of pectin, as I fervently scanned the groups of mums walking through the gates, desperately hoping that one my friends would come along and rescue me. I was being held hostage by my own politeness.

On her own, Claudia is rather dull, but the really irritating thing about her is that she is so absorbed in her own self, that she seems totally unaware that her cretin of a son terrorises all the children in his year and because she's the 'alpha mum' everyone is frightened of raising it with her (me included.)

There is a group of people that a clever mum would never go up against and they are the PTA and Claudia Greenacre is the head of the PTA.

As I stood, smiling, nodding and feigning an interest in fruit preserve, Claudia thankfully seemed to finally exhaust herself on the jam subject. Deciding to abruptly change the conversational course, she asked how Jamie was doing this year. I know that some mums are being polite and are genuinely interested in how well my son is progressing, but I still can't help feeling a little defensive when I hear it, as this question is normally posed in a very patronising manner. Giving my usual, stock answer, I said that Jamie was really enjoying school and was getting on better, as each year progressed. I was biting my lip not to say "How's Billy getting on ? Is he still barking like a dog for no apparent reason ?" When Claudia said in reply to my gush of pride for my son. "Yes, I thought he was doing well. Whenever Billy talks about Jamie, it's just as if he's one of the class."

Luckily, at that moment one of the administrators from the school office, came rushing up to Claudia with an impending cake sale emergency. Forcing a smile, I safely made my escape, before I told Greenacre where she could stick her jars of jam.

Standing out of sight around the corner, I started replaying the conversation back over in my head. I was still in a state of shock and a part of me was certain that I must have imagined such a backhanded compliment. As I mentally listened to it through again, the insult was definitely there. I have no doubt at all that Claudia expected me to be pleased that after four years, my son had finally gained her son's approval. But all I could think was 'what a bloody cheek!' That comment 'as if he's one of the class!!!' As opposed to what? A dog ? An alien ? I had to stop myself from walking back around the corner and shouting "at least my son has a diagnosis, what's your Billy's excuse ?"

Just as I started to feel the first pangs of a tension headache beginning a march across my forehead, I saw Jamie, with a face that mirrored my own. His teacher (Mr Rawlings,) walked next to him, had pretty much the same look. Mr Rawlings is a slight man with thinning sandy coloured hair, small round glasses and a penchant for beige corduroy trousers and sadly, he was looking even more troubled than normal. It never ends well, when Jamie and a teacher look at me like that.

As they stopped in front of me, the expressions on their faces said it all. Then his teacher uttered the six most terrifying words that any teacher could ever say "we need to have a chat." As Jamie went and sat down on a bench at the opposite end of the playground, Mr Rawlings said, in a lowered voice "Jamie said the F word today and he had to lose his afternoon play time." Staggered by what he had just said, I tried damage limitation, surely he had this wrong. "Did he say frig or frick ? He's heard it on the telly and might think it's OK to repeat those."

This is when the frown in his forehead deepened and he leaned in close, like he was closing a drugs deal. "No! It was the bad F word and he said he didn't hear it at school, but at home." I spluttered a defensive denial, which even I don't think I truly believed and then said "I'll go and talk to him. He'll lose his pocket money privileges and I can assure you that it won't happen again."

Turning on my heel and trying to muster as much dignity as possible, I marched over to where my son sat sulking. Seeing me, he stood up with a face like thunder and walked in front of me towards the gate, without a word. "Jamie" I said, putting a hand out to stop him and turned him around to face me. "You've let me down and you've let yourself down. I'm going to have to withhold your pocket money." He glared at me in silence, as I glared back, unable to believe what a position he had put me in. This is the kid who spells out the word 'H E L L' or 'H E C K' and I'm supposed to believe that he said the bad F word in public. Annoyed at his silence, I asked him "so what happened ?" He sighed and kicked at the pathway with his shoe, before raising his head and saying "we had to go and get our books and I said 'not those F'ing books again' except I said it the bad way and Dominic heard me and then he went and told the teacher." Jamie was acting like he was the injured party and the whole conversation seemed so surreal, it was one of those occasions when I really wished there was some sort of handbook for bringing up children. "I'm going to have to stop you watching all those comedy programmes you like. I thought I could trust you to hear the swearing without repeating it." His wounded pride was roused and he shot back "that doesn't stop me from hearing it in the playground does it ?"

Annoyed that I was having to justify myself, I said "if you hear it in school, why on earth did you tell the teacher that you've only heard it at home ?" He spoke slowly, as if I was an idiot and needed things spelling out clearly. "I couldn't say that. I didn't want to get my friends in trouble." Now I was really exasperated! "Right, so no grown up TV and no pocket money. What have you learned from all this ?" Without a hint of irony and with more sincerity than I have ever heard from him before, Jamie looked me right in the eye and said. "I've learned not to trust Dominic, he's a bloody grass." Sometimes, as a parent you have to turn your head away quickly, before your child sees you laugh.

Chapter Nine - So Good Safari

I was bound to uphold the no adult TV and pocket money rules, but luckily, I hadn't threatened to cancel tickets to a local safari park that I'd previously bought online. John had to work and the kids had really wanted to go. So, for some reason I had heard myself offering to take both children, on my own and I honestly can't think why. I've never taken them out on my own before, it's always seemed such a scary prospect.

Waking Hope up first, I said to her "what do you want to do at the park today?" Bouncing up and down excitedly, she said. "First, I want to feed Jamie to the lions and then, can we run over some monkeys, please Mummy?" I had a VERY bad feeling about the day out.

I had managed to prepare and pack a picnic, got two children washed and ready (honestly it's like herding cats) and after a mystery tour, courtesy of the Satnav. (I actually harbour a suspicion that our Satnav has Asperger's Syndrome too. It knows so much, but if you have to make a diversion, it fails to adjust and keeps repeating the way that it wanted to go originally,) we finally arrived at the safari park.

We did the usual things, went on the little boat, the little train and looked at the animals in the petting zoo. Once we'd finished, Jamie said that he wanted to go into the lorikeet house by himself. He assured me that it would be OK. He had been in with John several times and it was no big deal. I paid for the bird food, which was a little pot of syrupy stuff and then in he very bravely went, with the food held high.

Hope and I followed his progress from the outside and things seemed to be going well, as he got to the halfway point of the enclosure. Jamie had assured me that the birds come down one at a time and hover in front of the cup, daintily taking a little bit of the food at a time... Turns out, Jamie was talking rubbish!

Rather than Dr Doolittle, what happened next, was more like a scene from 'The Birds.' I could barely see Jamie, as a mass of colourful lorikeets suddenly descended on him. They weren't just hovering in front of the cup, they were actually landing on him with their sharp little talons.

The member of staff in the enclosure, was right at the other end, concentrating on taking money and handing out more food to other customers and I couldn't get in through the exit way, so all I could do was stand and watch, as his face turned a weird kind of beetroot colour.

I smiled in relief as I saw a family go over to him and I thought that at last, he had some help. Unfortunately, they decided to just stand there taking pictures of the 'amazing lorikeet boy.'

I heard him screaming "help me. Somebody help me" over the whirring and clicking of the cameras and have never felt so, utterly powerless. I did the only thing I could think of, I shouted to him "Jamie, keep calm and slowly put the cup on the floor."

As if by magic, the moment that the cup touched the floor, the birds surrounded the cup and left my poor little boy alone. He managed to get out of the exit, and I gave him a huge hug, as he fell into my arms. Bless him, he was pretty shaken, but he just kept saying, "How did you know that would work ? How did you know ?"

It was the only time that I could ever remember, when Jamie had acknowledged that I knew something that he didn't, so I was a little bit reluctant to tell him that it was just common sense and that the birds were after the food and not him, but I'm a little ashamed to say, that I just hugged him and said "it's just one of those things that a Mum knows."

Following the avian attack, we sought out the safety of our five door blue estate and despite being surrounded by lush green meadows, we ate our picnic right there in the car (because Jamie was scared of birds swooping down out of the sky to get at the food.) When two tiny stomachs (and one considerably larger one) had been satisfactorily filled with sandwiches, crisps, drinks, apples and chocolate cake, we headed up to the drive through safari.

The safari park section is always my favourite. It's the one area, where we don't have to deal with the public, the kids aren't running around everywhere and it means we survive the day and are nearly at the end and ready to go home. (More importantly, it also means that, once you start driving through the animals, there's no possibility of spending any more money.)

Listening to the accompanying CD, we drove past the giraffes and the zebras and I had to start shouting at the kids to turn their tablets off and start looking at the wonders of nature just outside of the window. "Humph" was the response I got, but I did hear them reluctantly turning their gadgets off.

Next was the rhino enclosure and that didn't raise any interest either. I was starting to get a bit annoyed that my efforts weren't being appreciated, but as we turned into the deer enclosure, they began to get excited. "Can we feed the deer Mummy ?" In that one sentence, I realised why they were so happy. They had found a way to spend money, even in the middle of the safari park. Finding my last two pounds in my purse, I bought two polystyrene cups of pellets, from a helpful lad in a wooden shed, surrounded by hungry deer.

I lowered the windows, as the kids tantalisingly waved their cups. Unfortunately, Jamie suffered a flashback, due to his PTLSD (Post Traumatic Lorikeet Stress Disorder,) when a giant deer, put his head in through the car window and took the whole cup out of Jamie's hand. He started screaming (Jamie, not the deer) and Hope threw her pellets all over the back of the car in shock.

Pushing the deer's huge face back out of the car, I raised the windows and we continued around the rest of the animals in silence and double quick time. I didn't even slow down for my favourite ever animals, the wolves.

I don't think I'll ever volunteer to take the kids on a day out without John, ever again.

Chapter Ten - Sleepless In Suburbia

I genuinely can't remember when I last had a lie in on a weekend. Before we had the kids, John would make me breakfast in bed every weekend. Sunday mornings were always my particular favourite, when we would pop to the newsagents (literally two doors away from our old house) and then sit with mugs of hot coffee, trying to solve the crossword puzzles, whilst the aroma of a slowly roasted dinner permeated the air.
Then, at bedtime we would take a giant bar of chocolate to bed with us and sit watching TV in bed, scoffing treats. That is not how Sundays go in our house now!

At six o'clock in the morning, there isn't the lovely sound of a cockerel crowing or church bells ringing to wake me up. My 'rude awakening' is usually courtesy of Hope. Most morning, she was suddenly sit upright and let the loudest fart in the world, reverberate throughout the bedclothes and sits there giggling to herself at how funny she is!

Whenever the kids awake, I always use the same tactic that they use in films, when dealing with a T-Rex. I figure, that if I don't move and keep my eyes closed, they won't see me and will move along past me. I don't know why I persist in this foolish notion, because it NEVER works... EVER!!!!

Hope was undeterred by my closed lids. "Wake up Mummy. It's morning time." Based on previous experience, I didn't even bother arguing that it was too early and she should go back to sleep, I just fumbled for the remote control and put on the first kids TV channel I could find.

I was just happily dozing back off to sleep, when the adverts came on and Hope's interest was firmly put back onto me. "You can't sleep. You're my Mummy!" I didn't even have time to query her insane logic, because the shouting had obviously woken the other light sleeping dinosaur and Jamie thundered in, bounced down onto the middle of the bed, wanting to know where his glasses and electronic tablet were and why I wasn't downstairs cooking breakfast.

Sleep laughed at me, as it danced off out of my reach and I consigned myself to the fact that I wouldn't see it again for at least another sixteen hours. John no longer had the luxury of being at home on Sundays, he has to work and so I had to make my own breakfast. I stumbled downstairs, with my hair sticking up like Russell Brand in the early days, followed by two squabbling children and made my way to the one thing that would make me feel human again… The kettle!

After the first sip of coffee, I started to feel so much better. I even managed to dish two bowls of cereal out (with no milk! Neither of them like milk in cereal. Apparently, putting milk on your cereal is odd) and collapsed onto the sofa with my coffee and burnt toast.

I spent a blissful morning catching up on my soaps, Hope decided she wanted to watch a DVD on the little TV which sits right next to the big TV in our living room, whilst Jamie seated himself in front of the PC in the far corner and refused to move, whilst he happily watched online video game tutorials.

It's a good job that I had become so adept at filtering out noise, because the cacophony of sound in our living room would drive you mad otherwise. We permanently have to keep the subtitles on the TV, because otherwise I wouldn't be able to keep track of what is going on in a programme, with all the background noise and chatter.

At twelve o'clock I managed to move away from the TV and found myself dazed and confused in the kitchen. John and I love a good roast, but the kids hate them. They don't like gravy. They moan about it every week and I end up having to throw away three quarters of the meal. It's not cheap to put a roast together and it takes me half a day of effort, just to be whined at and then I end up being forced to cook fish fingers about half an hour after, when they refuse to eat those dangerous and magical things, the ancients called 'vegetables.'

Some people often like to use the phrase "they'll eat when they're hungry," but clearly those people have never had a child with Autism. The very first time that I weaned Jamie onto solid foods with some mashed up apple, he turned his head away and cried. When he was two years old, I refused to cook him another meal until he ate the one I had put in front of him. He refused to eat for three days. He doesn't feel hunger, is sensitive to temperatures and so he has what I think of (and am in no way medically qualified, just a poor, put upon mother) as the 'Goldilocks Syndrome.' If something's too hot he won't touch it and then if it's too cold he won't touch it. This means he has about a minute in which his food is at just the right temperature. I long for the day when he asks me for a cooked breakfast or more roast potatoes for his Sunday dinner.

I was finding myself particularly annoyed with Jamie's attitude. He had been quite intimidating and obnoxious and even violent towards his little sister. I decided that it wasn't fair for her to be putting up with his ever escalating outbursts, so I tried to think what my parents did to me when I was his age. I could clearly recall being sent up to my bedroom and my mum shouting out "I've just rang the children's home and they said they're going to send a van out to come and get you. Do you want me to ring them back and tell them to cancel it ?"

I am thirty eight now and yet I can still clearly recall the panic and grief I felt at the thought of these strangers coming to collect me and take me away from my family. I would instantly break down, say I was sorry over and over and promise never to do anything naughty ever again.

Deciding that yes, it was cruel, but his behaviour was such that he needed a short, sharp shock treatment, I resolved to do the same thing.

Sometimes being a parent and having to do things for the greater good is hard, but you just have to remember why you're doing it and see it through. This, was one of those times.

Feeling slightly smug, I feigned anger and ordered Jamie up to his room for pushing Hope off her chair and shouted out to him. "I've just rang the children's home and they're going to send a van to come and get you. Do you want me to ring them back and tell them to cancel it ?" There was silence for a couple of seconds and I felt so proud of myself for remembering this failsafe method of parenting. I was just mentally preparing a blog about how I had cracked behaviour management, when his door opened and Jamie shouted out. "It depends. What's the food like ?"

I had to walk away at that point because I honestly didn't know if I was going to laugh, scream or cry and went to find a corner in which to do all three.

Later that night, as we settled down into bed, ready for sleep and exhausted from the long day. Jamie (who had long since calmed down) looked at me and said "I don't believe children's homes exist. I think you were just saying it to scare me. Show me proof." I spent an hour proving my point on various websites, but he didn't seem unduly worried. That's the problem in dealing with someone so logical, he knows very well, that this was one particular threat, I was never going to carry out. I was well and truly hoist by my own petard.

Chapter Eleven - A Very Humble Harvest

This morning, I went flying into Hope's nursery a veritable tornado of indignation. I was on a mission to avenge my hard done-by princess.

Normally, on a Tuesday morning, I am all sweetness and light when dropping her off, but today I had the nursery manager, Claire caught in the crosshairs and I was taking down a cretin called Kevin with the same bullet.

Hope only goes to nursery for three sessions a week and whenever she comes home, she's always upset about Kevin and the evil things that he does, simply to torment her. I do mention it to Claire, but she just looks at me in her lovely, polite manner and goes "alright, we'll keep an eye on it." Well I had finally had enough.

Hope came home from nursery saying that Kevin had kicked her and then stamped on her long blonde hair. So this was it. I wanted Kevin gone out of our lives forever. (Why don't they have the pre-school equivalent of a young offender's unit ?) I was going to demand that the nursery get rid of him once and for all and I wasn't going to listen to any of their excuses. It was time for action.

Barging past two mums with their babies strapped across their chests, who were stood yapping about their new organic eating plans. I marched right up to where Claire was sitting with a mound of salt dough and a mountain of various shaped cutters and with the might of justice behind me. I lifted my chin (in my best, no nonsense stance) and said "Claire. I've had enough. I want to make a formal complaint about Kevin. I will not send Hope here to be bullied and I will keep her out until he is made to leave."

Claire turned a deep crimson colour (she is just lovely and really hates any confrontation, even with toddlers) and said "I don't understand. What's happened ?"

I drew myself up to my fullest height (four feet, eleven inches) and said in a tone, used by newsreaders the world over to impart terrible news. "Kevin, kicked my daughter yesterday and stamped on her hair. Hope said that no one told him off and I've had enough of it. It's something every single day with that kid and I am not willing to put up with it any longer. I think you need to bring his parents in and tell them that he has to leave the nursery if he touches Hope again."

Sinking back down to my usual four feet ten inches, I held my breath and waited. "You're sure this happened yesterday ? At nursery ?" I was incensed that someone would question the word of my beautiful girl. "Yes. He did it yesterday. Hope doesn't tell lies." Claire looked really uncomfortable and I was certain that I had won the day with my ultimatum, when she uttered the words that took just seconds to make my world explode and left me feeling about ten inches tall.

"I'm sorry, but he couldn't have. Kevin's been at home with chickenpox, since last week."

I was SO embarrassed! Making my apologies and shooting threatening glances in Hope's direction, I left, with cheeks redder than even Claire's had been.

I didn't have time to dwell on my humiliation (though I did resolve to check out different pre-schools on the internet when I got home, as I didn't think I could look Claire in the eye ever again) as it was Jamie's harvest service at the church next door to where I had just dropped off Hope and embarrassed myself, like never before.

I had spent the previous night making a sheaf of wheat out of granary bread for Jamie's year group and despite the pressure I had put on myself, to get it just right, I was proud of the finished piece. We always had one at our school and I used to spend the whole service, looking at the giant bread and wishing I could eat it. I've never made one before and I was really proud of myself (I wasn't so proud of the way I'd been screaming in the kitchen last night, like Gordon Ramsey on a bad day, whenever anyone asked if I needed any help.) I had even made a little mouse to go on top. Jamie's headmistress promised to share the bread with the children at the end of the day (it almost made me forget my earlier shame. Poor Kevin! Perhaps I should make a sheaf of wheat for him.) I can't make cupcakes and I can't cook scrambled eggs, but I can bake bread like a professional. Out of the corner of my eye, I noticed one of the PTA brigade eyeing me with undisguised hostility, as I was asked to take a bow and the children clapped me.

Jamie had been totally unimpressed when I had shown him the sheaf, but when he came out of school at the end of the day, his friends all came running up to me, saying how much they loved the bread. Turning to Jamie, I said "so did you have any ?" He smiled and nodded and he said these amazing words, which, if I ever open my own bakery, I will use as a slogan. He said "I had some and I thought to myself, not bad bread." I did allow myself a small amount of satisfaction, because for Jamie, the words 'not bad bread' were a ringing endorsement indeed.

When I got home, I spent the rest of the morning, writing out lists for our forthcoming holiday and alternately finding myself bathed in a hot sweat of mortification at the memory of this morning's incident, which would always be known as 'Kevingate.'

Standing in a shadowy corner of the playground, I was desperately trying to dodge various members of the PTA, who were on the hunt for victims (I mean volunteers) for this week's bake sale. I emerged into the sunlight, just as Jamie and Mr Rawlings came meandering up to me as though they had all the time in the world. "Why don't you go and wait for Mummy on the bench ?" His teacher asked in an overly bright and reassuring way. Which as every parent knows, is code for "I need to talk alone to your Mummy, because you've done something terrible, because you're Mummy is an awful parent and we're deciding whether to inform social services or just bitch about her in the staff room, during every morning break time. I braced myself for his latest tale of temper and meltdowns, but instead he said, "Jamie is a little worried about the holiday you're going on."

I'm normally annoyed if someone can get something out of him that I can't, but I was so relieved that he hadn't punched someone that I couldn't really take in what Mr Rawlings was saying. (Jamie is retaliating to bullying in a physical manner at the moment. The other morning, I told him to make sure he kept his hands and his feet to himself. So he threw a shoe at someone, because that wasn't on his list of things not to do.) "He's been very quiet in class today and he confided that he's scared. I thought you could have a word with him this evening perhaps." I thanked his concerned teacher and went to find my son, who was sitting on a bench looking a little bit pale. I didn't say anything to him, but I could tell that he was expecting a lecture, so I just let him witter on about computer games until we got home. At tea time, he listlessly pushed his fish fingers around the plate and didn't even touch his sweet corn.

I waited until bedtime and then I pounced. "Jamie is there anything worrying you ?" He knew where I was going with this, but he still pretended that he didn't. He just kept staring at the TV, ignoring me. "Mate, Mr Rawlings said you told him you were worried about the holiday. Is that true ?" His eyes didn't drift from the TV, but he slowly nodded his head. "Why didn't you tell me ?"

With his unfailing Aspie logic to everything he shrugged his bony little shoulders. "There wasn't any point. You've paid for the holiday and we have to go whether I'm scared or not. You're not going to cancel something the family has been looking forward to, just for me." Jamie over thinks everything and lets reason stop him from talking about his problems or seeking help and this was a perfect example of that. I made him switch his tablet on and I showed him pictures of the holiday accommodation online. He was so much calmer afterwards. In fact, he even seemed quite excited about it. The best part, was that he slept soundly for the first time in days.

Chapter Twelve - Halloween Horrors

I had spent so long dreaming of this trip, that when we finally set off, it kind of felt a bit like an anti-climax. When I'd imagined the journey in my mind, it had been full of singing along to the radio and playing eye spy. The reality, was the kids sat in the back with their headphones on, ignoring us whilst watching a DVD and me constantly bickering with John over whether we'd remembered to shut the front door or not.

As a treat, I'd brought six different bags of sweets, to keep everyone happy. My particular fondness is for lemon sherbets and I was feeling quite a virtuous smugness because I'd bought a bag of sugar free sherbets, so there was no downside to these lemony treats and my mouth had been salivating over the mere thought of them for days. Everyone else hates them, so even better, I was going to have them all to myself. (It doesn't take much to keep me happy.)

Turning up the music, I tried to forget the pull of my possibly open front door and the urge to do a handbrake turn and go home to check and I found solace in a whole bag of sherbet lemons.

As we saw a sign, welcoming us to the New Forest, my stomach started gurgling and my insides sounded like a hot water bottle being swished around. It was when the noise of my stomach was louder than the song that was playing on the radio that I started to get a bit scared. A couple of minutes later, I started getting cramps and the need to go to the toilet hit me in waves of seriousness and terror. "What's wrong ?" Asked John, sensing that something really wasn't right. "I don't know" I said, clenching my lower muscles against another wave of pain. "I ate those sweets and now I really don't feel so good."

"I'll have a look to see if you're allergic to any of the ingredients" he said helpfully, as I dug my fingers into the steering wheel, praying for the power to hold on and not to have to pull over and embarrass myself in front of a curious, wild roaming pony. "Would you say that the amount of sweets you ate could be considered excessive ?" John queried. "Seeing as how I ate the whole bag by myself, I guess you could say that. Why ?" If he was trying to make a point about my weight, whilst I was in pain, I was going to divorce him the moment the holiday was over. "It says on the back of the bag ?" He said, pausing for dramatic effect, as my stomach gurgled ominously. "Excessive consumption may result in laxative effects."

When your body is suffering from 'laxative effects,' being consumed by worry, really isn't going to help with your already, pressing symptoms. I'm not proud of what I did in the first public toilet that I found and I will never show my face in there again, but I just wanted to try and get to our holiday apartment, before the full effects of a whole bag of lemon laxatives took hold.

After a three hour car journey (that was literally touch and go,) we finally made it to the ferry port and following a tense half hour filled with. "Where's the ferry ? Why aren't we going ? Why's the ferry running late ? What time will we get there ? Are all these cars going as well ? How will they fit us all on ? Where are the toilets ? I'm bored! Can we go home ? Can I have a toy and a magazine on the ferry ? What will happen if the boat starts to sink ? Will there be enough lifeboats for everyone on board ?" We were thankfully given the go ahead to drive aboard the huge white, Solent going vessel.

We visit the island at least four times a year, so I know full well, how the children go crazy the moment we board the ferry. After all that time, cooped up in the car, they go off like a balloon when you let go of it and watch it fly around the room, until it runs out of air (I was trying my level best not to do my own impression of a loose balloon, complete with sound effects.)

This time I was prepared for them. I really didn't want to be roaming aimlessly around the ship with them for forty five minutes or spend all of our holiday money in the little onboard shop, before we even got to the Isle of Wight. As we took our seats, I produced two brand new games for their DS.' They'd cost me the best part of sixty pounds (roughly about the same price as two coffees and a packet of crisps on the ferry,) but to keep them entertained for the whole duration of the crossing, that had to make them worth every penny.

Usually, we stay in a caravan on a holiday park, but this time we were staying somewhere far more special and this was the cause of Jamie's concern. We had managed to book the only apartment in a beautiful castle and that included the night of Halloween. The castle is open to the public during the day, but after four pm, it would only be us left in the grounds and that was going to be an exciting privilege.

Winding our way up towards the hill where the castle lay, trees threw their leaves in our path and I started to feel a little uneasy (and not from the effects of the sweets this time, at least I didn't think it was) about our choice of holiday location. As we finally reached the ancient portcullis, we were greeted by Stella the housekeeper. "Welcome to the castle" she smiled warmly.

The sky had turned as grey as Stella's hair, promising a torrential downpour and visitors were beginning to leave in droves. Giving us the code for the modern gate, which stood just in front of the medieval gateway, Stella ushered us towards our apartment.

We were apparently staying in an old stable block, which had been refurbished (using only the best décor that John Lewis could provide) and Stella proudly presented us with a hamper of red wine, crumpets, fresh bread, fluffy scones, fresh extra thick cream, a block of mature cheese and a particularly fine strawberry and champagne preserve, that even Claudia Greenacre would approve of. "Thank you so much Stella" I gushed, trying not to sound scared out of my wits at the spooky atmosphere. "I'm sure we'll be very happy."

The children ran to find their bedroom and filled the apartment with noise and laughter, which still didn't alleviate my feelings of being watched by some unseen presence, which I really hoped would prove to be a cat hiding under the sofa.

As soon as Stella said her goodbyes (and no cat had revealed itself,) I ran around turning on all the lights, no longer worried about what anyone thought. I was uncomfortable and I couldn't admit it in front of the children, but I wanted to go home. "Come on" said John "let's go and get something to eat. It's been a long day." Glad for any excuse to leave, I grabbed our coats and we headed out. The kids hadn't wanted to get back in the car, but I was so relieved to be outside with people once more. I really didn't know how I was going to get through the next four nights.

We have a bit of a tradition that on our first night on holiday, we always get fish and chips from our favourite takeaway in Sandown and we sit and eat them on the seafront. So, thirty minutes later we found ourselves eating our food in the car, overlooking the water.

It's my favourite place in the whole world. There's something so calming about listening to the waves, lapping against the shore and watching the tankers and cruise ships slowly making their way to exotic locations, that couldn't compete with how beautiful the Isle of Wight is (in my unbiased opinion.)

Being children, the kids weren't as happy as me to sit and look at the scenery for hours, so as soon as the last chip had been consumed, they wanted to go for their obligatory walk around the arcade on the pier and spend a fortune of our money, by stealth, taking a pound here, then a pound there, so that I wouldn't realise how much we had spent until it was too late. Hope loves being on the pier, whereas Jamie prefers to shuffle behind me, terrified of the scary zombie type games, but the lure of winning is stronger than his overall fear of monsters.

Jamie's favourite thing is the claw machines. I have lost count of the number of times that I have failed to win him a particular toy and then failed to bribe the staff into letting me buy one from them. Every visit to an arcade with Jamie, usually ends in me having to scour the internet until I find exact same toy, and then paying an extortionate amount for the toy plus the delivery. Jamie will cry and whine for at least a week until it comes and then roughly fifty minutes after it has been delivered, he will (without fail) forget all about it and the toy will find its way into a bin liner and will be stored in the loft.

We have quite a collection of plush toys. Once, at a service station, we managed to grab a toy, but it was too big to fit down the chute. No one onsite had a key for the machine and, whilst we were in Exeter at the time, the nearest engineer was apparently in Newcastle. I refused to leave the services and in the end, one of the members of staff managed to insert some metal rods in between the sections of glass and forced the toy out. My kids were quite impressed with me that day for not backing down. That particular toy (that we couldn't leave without) is currently residing in our loft.)

Luckily, this time I managed to win Jamie the toy that he had his eye on and Hope won a skateboard key ring in the two pence machines, so she was ecstatic with her prize (which cost roughly seven pounds to win and probably would have cost two pounds fifty to buy in a shop down the road.)

With two fed and happy children, clutching their hard fought for prizes, we drove back towards our own private castle.

When I initially booked our holiday, I thought it would be a huge honour to have such a historical palace all to ourselves. I had visions of the children dressed as knights, running around on the green. I thought that I would enjoy walking around the grounds on my own private ghost hunt, especially at Halloween.

I have run ghost hunts for eleven years and I didn't think anything could scare me anymore, I've pretty much seen it all. As someone who loves history and the Stuarts in particular, it was such an honour for me to be able to stay in the very same place that King Charles I was held captive, before he was taken to London for his execution. Ever since we'd made the booking, I had envisaged night time walks across the battlements and having the time and peace to soak up the atmosphere. I was even hoping that I might even manage to spot a ghost or two.

As we drove up the hill, the battlements looked inky black and the sky was so much darker than when we had set out to get our food. The castle was deserted now and because there were no street lights this high up, it was difficult to see the numbers on the combination lock at the gateway. My fingers fumbled in the cold, but I managed to finally open the gates and waved John through. Closing up behind me, I jumped back in the car (praying that my husband wouldn't try to be funny and drive off to the apartment on the other side of the castle, leaving me alone in the darkness. I didn't need any further laxative effects, I'd had more than enough for one day. It's usually the kid's explosive bottoms that we have to worry about on long trips.) Luckily for me, John wasn't feeling very humorous either, as he stared into the darkness beyond the gateway. The kids fell uncharacteristically quiet in the back, mutely hugging their toys and even John (who hadn't batted an eyelid when my emergency c section went wrong) looked scared.

Pulling into our allocated parking bay, we were out of that car and up the stairs in double quick time. The wind whistled through the trees. The leaves made a constant shrieking roar and a sign on the side of the building, stated that there were seventeen different bat species living in the surrounding walls. I had to be an adult and let the kids go in front of me, but it took all my will power not to trample on them, as I ran for safety.

Desperately trying to assure the kids that all was well, we put the TV on and lit the fire. Sitting down on the comfy blue sofa with a warm mug of coffee in my cold little hands, I was still a little jumpy, but tried to focus on the children and the soap opera, that I was only half watching on the tiny little screen.

Finishing my drink, I put my empty mug in the sink, pulled back the mullioned windows and peered outside. I have often heard people use the phrase 'pitch black,' but I had never truly appreciated what it meant before. I couldn't even see where the ramparts ended and the sky began. The only alleviation of the all-consuming darkness, was a small light bravely shining in the gatehouse, which cast a tiny pool of light about a foot in circumference around itself. I vowed that if I saw anything move in that miniscule beam of light, I wouldn't stop to ask questions, I would get the kids into the car and be on the first ferry home. John would have to make sure that he moved pretty fast, because I wouldn't stop to wait for him.

My exterior may have exuded calm, but when John inadvertently switched the hall light off, I screamed like an eight year old girl at a boy band concert.

John thought it was hilarious that I, the great ghost hunter, was so terrified of a pastel painted apartment. Things really weren't working out quite how I thought they would. Far from roaming around the battlements, I was holed up in the apartment like an agoraphobic, in a well-furnished prison without any bars. I was even too frightened to look out of the windows. Heaven only knows what it would be like at Halloween.

Chapter Thirteen - It's Beginning To Look A Lot Like Christmas

We woke to our first morning in the castle and at sunrise, it really was beautiful and peaceful (and a little less ominous.) After breakfast, we got in the car and went to the dinosaur museum (Hope's choice,) then we did a spot of shopping at the many stores in Newport (Jamie's choice.)

When we stopped at the supermarket to get something to eat for tea, I sent John and the kids down to the frozen food aisle, whilst I sneakily nipped to the medicine and vitamin aisle.

I am very much against the idea of giving my children medication to control their condition, but Jamie has been very anxious on this holiday and it was starting to cause me concern. He keeps saying things like "my feet are on the wrong way" or holding onto his ears in case they fall off (he learned about Van Gogh in school this term!) I decided that it was time to get a little herbal help (not the illegal kind.)

I had heard about these sweets you could buy in supermarkets and pharmacies. They simply contain essence of flowers and some might argue that it's nothing more than a placebo, but they're supposed to have a calming effect and they have no side effects, so I decided that I had nothing to lose and they might just help him to calm down. I grabbed Jamie a tin of the orange flavour pastilles and didn't say anything to him at the checkout.

Jamie's anxiety seems to get worse when we're on back roads because he doesn't know where he is or where he is going and he doesn't have faith in us, that we know which direction we're driving in. Normally, we would let him sit with the map, but the one we have, doesn't show the roads of the Isle of Wight so he was really struggling.

In his seat in the back of the car, Jamie started holding his head and was getting upset. Seizing my chance, I said "why don't you try one of these sweets ?" He didn't even reach out to take one, he just looked me in the eye and said. "That's not a sweet. We went down the sweet aisle and I didn't see you pick those up. So you're lying, because they're not sweets at all." Trying not to laugh at his obviously heightened suspicions and observational skills (for a boy that didn't notice for three weeks that we no longer had a dog,) I said "they're special calm down sweets, for when you're feeling worried or upset." Again, he didn't go to take one, but at least he'd stopped holding his head. "What you mean like medicine ? I can't believe you're trying to give me medicine ? Are you trying to drug me ? I could have you arrested for that."

I spent the rest of the journey, explaining about how they were made from flowers and totally safe etcetera and eventually (after looking them up on internet) he tried one. Fortunately, he liked the taste and he seemed a bit calmer, so I'm taking that as a win (for now.)

As a treat to lighten the mood a little, we went to our favourite garden centre, where they have a 'Christmas World' and it's become part of our yearly tradition to visit. It signals the start of the Christmas period for us. Unlike the rest of my family I have OCD (Obsessive Christmas Disorder) and I look forward to going to Christmas World all year round.

This year however, there was something new. In the middle of the garden centre, was a giant inflatable snow globe. I must admit, I didn't need much persuading when the kids asked to have a go. Two minutes later, we were playing in the fake snow in the middle of a huge snow globe, in the middle of a garden centre. Jamie was making snow angels, Hope was throwing snow balls, John was chucking snow around on all of us and I was singing the chorus of 'Let it Go,' (because let's face it, that's the only bit anyone really knows,) pretending I had summoned a snow storm (and hoping I couldn't be heard by the other shoppers, but unable to stop myself all the same.)

After five minutes of the most fun I've had in years, we posed for photos and reluctantly left the dome. After choosing our favourite, we came away with a picture of us covered in snow that we would treasure for years to come (and our throats full of fake snow that would probably last just as long.)

Despite all the fun, we made sure that we were back inside the castle grounds by four pm, because it starts to get dark early and none of us wanted to be outside the apartment at nightfall. The kids had brought their knight costumes and they were practising their sword fighting on the green, which they really loved, right up until the point where Hope got a bit overexcited by the authenticity of it all and started to really attack Jamie with her sword. At four thirty, we had managed to stop Jamie from crying and were all safely ensconced in our pastel coloured apartment. It was an unspoken rule that neither one of us wanted to be have to drive back in through the courtyard in the dark again. I spent yet another night, lying in bed, hoping not to hear anything go bump in the night.

All too soon, the safety of morning arrived and it was Halloween!!!! The time of year when the veils between the two worlds is supposed to be at their thinnest and ghosts enter our realm. (Or, in reality, it's when tiny muggers dress up and demand sweets and money with menaces.) Jamie is absolutely terrified at the prospect of spending Halloween inside one of Britain's most haunted castles. I did assure him that, on the upside, at least we wouldn't have to deal with any trick or treaters, but that didn't seem to lighten his spirits (pardon the pun) at all.

I left the family having breakfast, as I went for an early morning walk around the battlements and stopped at the top, overlooking the portcullis at the main entrance to the castle. From such a high, solitary vantage point, I had wanted to try and imagine the soldiers that had walked the same stone before me, defending the island from Spanish or French invaders, but actually, the minute I got up there, I got distracted by looking at the people walking their dogs around the moat outside, yawning and following their beloved pets around with little plastic bags. So once again, I failed to find the magic I was expecting.

As I headed back to the warmth of the apartment, I passed the old guards house, next to the impressive (and reputedly, haunted) stone gateway.

My heart lurched as I heard voices coming from inside the locked building. The voices were speaking English, but they had distinctive Spanish accents and they sounded angry. I began to run towards the apartment, terrified of the Spanish spectres. I rounded the last corner before the safety of our rooms, when I literally fell into the arms of one of the staff, who had just finished bringing the donkeys in from the field outside. "Maria" I yelped at the startled girl, as I fought to get my breath back. "I've just heard voices coming from inside the old guard's room. But it's locked and no one else is here." Slowly picking some stray strands of straw from the sleeves of her purple fleece, Maria laughed at me. I mean like, really laughed! "The voices you heard are coming from the film that we show in there during the day. It automatically comes on in the mornings and then runs on a loop. That's what you heard."

Feeling like a complete idiot, I walked away, dragging my wounded pride with me, all the way up the stairs to our apartment, resolved to spend the rest of the day inside the apartment, so that I couldn't see the staff laughing at me.

Unfortunately, my family refused to have mercy on me and forced me out of the front door, so that we could go and visit our favourite dairy shop. It is miles in the wrong direction and it would be far easer and cheaper to grab our milk in the supermarket, but they have calves at the dairy that you can go and pet and it's just a lovely place to visit, plus the milk in the supermarket never tastes quite the same as it does when it comes from the dairy. As well as the milk, and a loaf of overpriced crusty bread, we bought two perfect, giant orange pumpkins, some tea light candles and a box of cooking matches.

Pleased with our purchases, we made our way back to the castle. Jamie had chewed on one of his calm down sweets and was seemingly quite happy. Although his anxiety had been reduced, his ability to annoy his sister, unfortunately wasn't. Hope was happily singing away in the back of the car to Katy Perry. She's turning into quite the little Katycat and knows the words to all the songs across three albums. Today, she was singing along to 'Hot N Cold' (or 'Changey Mind,' as she likes to call it!) Unfortunately, the radio station were playing a censored version of the song and so when KP's voice was blanked out on a certain naughty word, we all quite clearly heard Hope sing the word 'bitch.' I didn't think anything of it, but Jamie was absolutely incensed. He turned to Hope and said "Father Christmas won't bring you any presents now, because you said a bad word. That means you're on the naughty list."

Within seconds, the happy atmosphere had evaporated and Hope was in floods of tears. Jamie was shouting at her that it was all her own fault and I was shouting at Jamie not to upset his sister and trying to calm her down. The thing is though, that from Jamie's point of view he was simply being logical and right (as usual) and I just confused him by telling him off. As things began to calm down, I explained that if he can see his sister getting upset, he should just stop arguing, even when he believes he is in the right (I don't think for a minute, that he will be able to do this.) I also assured Hope that Santa would understand that she was just singing along to a song and not being intentionally naughty.

Walking back into the castle, we could see a group of people standing around two men in Dickensian attire in the middle of the green. We went over to take a look and ended up staying to watch their performance. It was all going well, until one of the men said. "This is said to be one of England's most haunted castles. Up in the gatehouse is a particularly malevolent spirit and under that yew tree, lurks an evil spirit." I turned around to catch such a look of terror on Jamie's face that I knew we'd be packed up and on that ferry home within half an hour. I whispered to him that none of what the men were saying was true and it was all done to scare the children for Halloween and he instantly calmed down. If there's one thing you can count on, it's Jamie's love of feeling superior and the more the men continued to spin their gory tales, the more Jamie enjoyed the fact that the other kids were being duped, but he alone knew the truth. For a child who doesn't believe anything I say, Jamie is sometimes very willing to trust me, when it's what he wants to hear.

Inwardly hating the actors, I led the family back to our apartment. (By this point, we were so scared of being out in the dark, we were coming in earlier and earlier.)

Sat around the pine kitchen table, the kids had fun carving their pumpkins and we proudly displayed them in the windows for all the visitors to marvel over. Normally we do this for fun, but silently I think we were all hoping that they really would ward off any evil spirits that lurked outside (and I wasn't talking mothers or mother in laws here.)

At seven o'clock, when darkness had descended all around us in our hilltop fortress, the apartment's landline phone started to ring. I picked up the receiver and said "hello" but there was no reply, which was really unnerving. After about thirty seconds I heard a click and the call ended. I mean REALLY! That's just what you want to happen on Halloween, when you're the only people in an eerie medieval castle isn't it ? I couldn't even say anything about it, because the kids were both sat there looking terrified due to the spooky night anyway. I instinctively rose to the window and as I peeked outside, I saw that the light in the gatehouse wasn't on. "Probably one of the staff forgot to turn it on" said John in his usual unflustered manner and three minutes later, John and Jamie were striding out into the pitch black night with their hoods pulled firmly up over their heads and armed with nothing but a tiny torch each. I've never been more proud of them, than I was at that moment. I certainly wouldn't have ventured out into that darkness, even if there was a million pounds waiting for me in the gateway.

The silent phone calls continued every twenty minutes, with the same conclusion. After the fourth ring, I was really agitated and unable to hide it any longer. "Who the hell is this ? Like getting your kicks by frightening people at Halloween do you ? Just so you know, I'm going to call the police, you pervert." There was silence for a couple of seconds before I heard a polite lady's voice say, "It's me Stella, the housekeeper for the apartment. Are you OK ?" Embarrassed for the second time in one day, I stuttered "oh Stella, I'm so sorry. We've been having these nuisance phone calls all evening."

"Yes, I should have told you about that." She sounded apologetic, but I was just happy that the calls weren't the beginning of a horror film scenario, where some psychopath targets a lone family in a medieval castle at Halloween. (Not that I ever over react of course.) "It's a telemarketing company ringing through an automated system," she continued, "apparently they block their number, so there's no way of stopping it and several of the other holidaymakers had complained about it. Apart from that, is everything OK ?"

"Oh yes" I lied "We're all very comfortable." I wished her a good night, sounding as self-assured as I could, but I didn't even bother putting the kids into their room. We all slept in our bed. Safety in numbers!

Chapter Fourteen - All At Sea

As soon as he woke up, the first thing that Jamie said was, "I can't believe it. We actually survived and we're still alive." Until then, I don't think I really quite appreciated, just how seriously worried he must have been about last night bless him.

I don't think we've ever been so thrilled to make the journey home from a holiday before. We sat in the lane waiting to be loaded onto the ferry and the kids began to fidget almost immediately. It's the only downside to a holiday on the island, waiting for the ferry and then actually being on board the ferry.

Jamie is terrified of the water and although I've tried to explain that if we sank, there will be a ferry in each of the ports either side of us and a lifeboat only seconds away, ready to come to our rescue. (Not to mention the two marinas at either side which are filled with boats that could help us,) he's still petrified. The only other thing he hates, is sitting in the car waiting for the ferry. We were the last car waved aboard and the relief to be on our way home was palpable.

Unfortunately, being the last car loaded on, meant that we were the last people up on deck and there were no seats left by the time we got up on deck. Finding, a spare window at the bottom of the stairs, we awkwardly sat down and hoped that the crossing wouldn't take too long. The thrill of the new DS games had worn off, by all the time we'd spent hiding in the castle.

As we were just about to turn towards the port for the final leg of the journey, we suddenly stopped. Ever the twitchy little rabbit, alert to sudden danger, Jamie instantly started panicking, "why are we stopping ? What's going on ? Are we sinking ? Is the ferry broken ? Can we go and find a safety raft ? What's happening ?" Laughing at his little worried face, I stroked his hair and inwardly wished that I hadn't left his calm down sweets in the glove box of the car. "We're just waiting for the other ship to pull out of the port. They're obviously just running late. Nothing's wrong. It's happened before, it's just that you've normally got your head in your DS and you haven't noticed it."

We sat waiting for the vessel that was in dock to move, but it didn't and all of a sudden our ship started to turn, setting the car alarms off on the decks down below, by its extreme and unexpected movement. An ominous bing bong noise sounded through the ferry, whilst ears everywhere turned to listen, all through the boat you could hear people shushing each other, so they didn't miss the announcement. "Good morning ladies and gentlemen. I'm afraid I have some bad news for you." Jamie mutely turned towards me, shooting me accusing glances that suggested he would never believe a word I uttered, ever again. "The ship that is currently in port, is unable to move. We have several engineers working on it, trying to move it out of the way and in the meantime, we will stay in the Solent and wait." The unanimous groan that reverberated around the ship was clearly audible and everyone tried to amuse themselves and their children. No one knew how long we would be waiting for, which isn't an easy thing to explain to two Aspie kids.

John heard that free refreshments were being handed out and took Hope to investigate, leaving me with a red faced, teary eyed little boy. "I spy with my little eye" I began and saw that I was drawing his interest, despite his best efforts to remain sullen. "Something coloured green and blue." Looking around the stairwell and then out of the huge, ferry window, Jamie said "the sea ?"

"Correct. Your go." He started to chuckle and tried to think of something suitably difficult for me to guess. "I spy with my little eye" he said "something coloured red."

"That sign ?" Jamie shook his head, looking quite smug at my inability to guess his clue. "The fire extinguisher ?"

"Yes" he said, pleased that he had managed to confuse me for a second. "Your turn Mummy."

"I spy with my little eye, something coloured blue and green."

"The sea ?" He asked.

"Yes, your go." By the time John and Hope returned with two coffees and two bottles of water, I had managed to get Jamie to guess 'the sea' around six times and his eyes were now watering from laughter, instead of tears. With my boy, distraction is always a good method, for making him forget his worries. Hope joined in the fun, as John sat sipping his coffee and pretending that he didn't know us. Silliness kept them both entertained for about twenty minutes, but as the ideas for further clues started to whither and the hilarity of me saying 'green and blue' had worn off, all heads inevitably turned back towards the ship that was still firmly staying in port.

Luckily, John realised that the ship had free WiFi and even more luckily, he had a full battery on his mobile phone. The kids, settled down happily watching videos of their favourite programmes on the tiny little screen and we were able to exchange worried glances over their heads.

Sometimes, it's hard being the grown up and having to exude outward calmness for your kid's sake, when all you want to do is run around the ship screaming and trying to rip your own clothes off, letting your claustrophobia and panic run wild. The ominous bing bongs sounded and once again they drew everyone's attention, we all hoped for good news. "Ladies and gentlemen, this is your captain speaking. I'm afraid to say that at this time, I have no further updates for you. Engineers are still working hard to move the other ship out of the way, but at the moment we have no timescale for how long this will take. Once again we are sorry for this delay and would like to remind you that free refreshments are available from our shop."

People passed us on their way to the toilets and one middle aged woman walked by and said "I feel so sorry for those of you with children," with a self-satisfied grin that confirmed all she felt was smugness, not sympathy and was off to settle down with a paper and a glass of wine, content to wait hours for the other ferry to be moved if needed. I can honestly say, that I hated that cheerful little woman.

Another forty five minutes passed in this way, with everyone getting more irritated, except for our kids who were glued to the little mobile phone screen, totally oblivious to the stressful situation going on all around them. There had been no WiFi at the castle and they were just thrilled to be connected to the world wide web once more. After what seemed hours, the bongs resounded through the ship once more and we all listened, hoping for good news, but concerned because we could clearly see that the other vessel had still not left the port. "Ladies and gentlemen. We have taken the decision to perform our emergency berthing procedure and I have to tell you that although we have not tried this for many years, we feel that we are left with no choice. We should be alongside in half an hour and ready to disembark you all within fifty minutes."

The mood on board was lightened considerably, but me being the worrier that I am, all I could hear was the captain's words stating that this was an emergency and they hadn't tried the procedure in years. I started to think of all the disaster movies I'd watched over the years and idly wondered whether I should ring my Dad to tell him I loved him, just in case I never got the opportunity to do so again.

For the first time ever, I was thankful that we had been the last car to board the ferry, this meant that we would be the last to disembark and I certainly wouldn't have wanted to be the first one to test the emergency berthing procedure. (At least this emergency berthing procedure wouldn't leave me with a train wreck for a body, like the last time I had an emergency 'birthing' procedure.)

Everyone had migrated towards the lounge that overlooked the port. Some people were filming the event on their mobiles and I couldn't help but imagine them all ending up on the internet, with the headlines 'Tragic footage filmed minutes before terrible accident on board cross Solent Ferry,' all the people stuck in port who were waiting, had gotten out of their cars and lined the fence along the jetty, as they would if the Queen herself were on board, or some terrible disaster were about to unfold. (I really do think Jamie might get his tendency to be overdramatic from me.) Men in hard hats and high visibility jackets were running up and down the harbour and we all watched in silence as they attached two makeshift roadways to the ship.

When we were finally secured alongside the port, everyone clapped and cheered and the men in hard hats looked a little relived, but still concerned. There were clusters of them standing around, which worried me further.

Following the final announcement, everybody walked slowly down to their cars, anxious to be heading home, but worried about driving off of the ship. There was no way, that John was going to get his mobile phone back, so the kids didn't put up a fight, as we buckled them into their seats. I was so scared as I sat there behind the steering wheel, I even started to worry that I might faint (whilst all the time, telling the kids how lucky we were to be having this adventure.)

Cars began to move in front of us and as I summoned up the courage to drive forward, I realised that the line had stopped. A Nissan Micra had got stuck at the bottom of the steep ramp and we had to wait a further twenty minutes for it to be moved, I could feel my anxiety rising by the minute. We had been on board the ship for precisely three hours and we had a long three hour drive ahead of us. The other cause for concern, was my children's short and fickle memories. I knew full well, that they wouldn't forget this problem with the ferry and it might be another twenty years before I could persuade them to get onboard a boat again. I opened the glove box and slipped one of Jamie's 'happy sweets' into my mouth.

Finally the Micra was moved and all too soon, it was our turn to drive off. After all the fear and the buildup, we drove off without incident and I had to stop myself from pulling over, getting out of the car, falling to the ground on my knees and kissing the solid earth beneath me, Pope style.

It was the first time we had ever returned home from the island in the dark. Instead of unpacking, we raced around, getting tea ready for the children, whilst they frantically switched the internet on and made themselves comfortable, oblivious to all the work of unloading the car and unpacking, that went on all around them.

Tonight was the first time I can ever remember, being relieved to see the orange streetlights outside our house. Even better, there were actual people walking up and down the road, which made me feel quite emotional. (I wanted to run out and hug them, but I most likely would have ended up getting punched or mugged, so I wisely decided against it.) Instead of a relaxing holiday, we came home feeling like people who had survived a traumatic event, rather than ending up peaceful and rested.

I thought that being at home, tucked up in our own beds would be calming. I also thought that after the journey home, the kids would have been tired and gone to sleep earlier. On both of these counts (as so often happens,) I found I was wrong…

Our kids have always gone to sleep in our bed and then, when they are finally asleep, one of us carries them into their own beds. Sometimes we time it wrong, or make a noise, mid-transportation and then they wake up and we have to put them back in our bed and start the process all over again. It's tiring and inconvenient sometimes, but it's the only thing that works (for our children.) It is getting a bit difficult for me to carry Jamie into his room, because he's only about six inches shorter than me, so it's a struggle to say the least. I invariably end up hitting his head on the door frame or catching his legs on the heater at the top of the stairs.

It doesn't matter how lovely a day we've had, at night time, I always end up shouting at Jamie and feeling like the worst parent in the world. Every night is the same. It's like Groundhog… erm Night!

You see, the thing that both amuses and irritates me in equal measure is Jamie's complete inability to moderate his volume. If our lives depended on us hiding in silence, I swear he wouldn't be able to do it. He honestly cannot whisper. He might try, but by the end of the sentence he's right up there at full volume again.

Tonight was murder. Each time that Hope started drifting off to sleep, Jamie would wake her up with his verbal diarrhoea. Another problem, is that he has no idea where his limbs are. (For someone who seemingly has no idea, he seems to have an unerring ability to whack Hope with his hands, arms and feet at every occasion,) which causes yet another temper tirade (from me.) Bedtime always ends with me being annoyed, Jamie annoyed, John tired, Hope upset and the neighbours no doubt muttering about whether to call Childline. Luckily, because he has a rubbish short term memory, every morning when he wakes up, he's forgotten all about the night before.

We were all cuddled up in bed, thankful to be home at last, when a slimming advert came on TV. Jamie turned to look at me and said "have you ever thought of joining a slimming club ?" Pointing to my stomach, he said "I think there's about a stone you need to lose, right there." Slow to come to my own defence, I spluttered "the reason I have a bit of a stomach, is because I had to have two caesareans, carrying you and your sister." I thought this might earn me an apology, but he muttered "well that's no excuse not to try." John shook his head in disbelief and said "You've got an awful lot to learn about women, if you ever want to get married mate."

Chapter Fifteen - Middle Age Dream

Finally after a three year wait, the day I had waited for, for three years had finally arrived. I would be in the same room as the most beautiful woman in the world (in my humble opinion anyway.) I was going to see KATY PERRY (cue the hysterical screaming!!!!!!!!)

At four pm precisely, I was parked outside my friend Emily's work, ready to drive straight to Birmingham (the farthest I have ever been from my children.) It was a good job that I had the driving to focus on, because I would have been a nervous wreck otherwise.

We made such good time, munching sweets and singing along to my Katy Perry CDs that we decided to stop and get something to eat in a services about fifteen miles away from the concert venue. Virtually everyone in that services was about thirteen years of age, accompanied by their mums and wore headbands with cat ears on. Feeling very old and also very happy that my cat eared headband was in the car, we got something to eat and I managed to force down about three chips (after spending a fortune on the sorry excuse for a meal) and before too long, we were back on the road again.

Sat in the arena, waiting for the concert to begin, I checked my phone for the hundredth time since we left, in case John had rung or text and as soon as I knew that there hadn't been any child related emergencies, I was free to hyperventilate in excitement about Katy Perry being right in front of me (give or take thirty feet.) Each time the support group (who were trying their level best to entertain people, who really didn't want to see them and just wanted Katy,) started a new song, I would tut and roll my eyes. Their half hour set seemed to go on forever and after waiting so long, I was beginning to lose patience (Once again, I wonder where the kids get it from !) Finally, we were sincerely told that they loved us all and that we were the best crowd they had ever sung for and then thankfully, they went.

The lights in the arena all went out and after a couple of minutes, several dancers in neon costumes walked out on to the stage and the crowd screamed in anticipation. A large pyramid/prism opened up to reveal... nothing inside, then it slowly closed again. I don't think I even allowed myself to blink as I waited to see Katy Perry in the flesh.

For a second time, the pyramid opened and this time, she was there, standing right in the middle of it. The arena erupted in applause and I screamed like a Beatles fan in the old news reels, when girls are fainting and crying like they've just had some sort of religious experience. She looked like she had been photo shopped, she really was as perfect as I'd imagined.

The concert passed in a blur of colour and energy and of course, amazing vocals. The only sad bit was when she sang Hope's favourite song and I wished my daughter had come with us to see it. Although it really was fantastic and I had waited for so long, I did feel a slight sense of disappointment that I couldn't go and meet her after and as close as she was, it still felt too far, in a funny way, it felt as if I was watching her on the TV. It didn't seem real. This, I realised, was how everything seemed to Jamie, nothing ever lived up to the hype and everything was always an anti-climax.

We got back home at two am and although I had to be up at six in the morning to start getting the kids ready for school and nursery, sleep eluded me. My ears were ringing and every time I closed my eyes, I saw the concert again, behind my tightly shut lids. It wasn't going to be pretty, when that alarm went off, but on balance, totally worth it. For once in my life, I had done something really fun, for me and I had loved every second of it and after checking on my sleeping children, I kissed my sleeping husband on his forehead, for being so good to me.

Chapter Sixteen - Diving Out Of My Comfort Zone

When you know about Autism, it is said that you can have a problem, where you see Autism everywhere and you end up diagnosing everyone's children (in your head obviously, it would make for one awkward coffee morning if you smilingly, said "you know your little Johnny's got Autism don't you ?")

Now I've been very careful, not to fall into this trap, but whilst I was watching Peppa Pig with Hope, I suddenly realised, that Peppa's brother George has serious speech delay, because for at least the last four years that I'd been watching Peppa, that little boy pig has only ever said the word 'dinosaur' and has an overwhelming dinosaur fixation. (Idly, wondered whether to email the programme makers to see if I'm right.)

Even though I have two children with Asperger's Syndrome and have been as Asperger friendly as possible, for the last nine years, I still sometimes, inexplicably forget who my children are and how literally they take everything and I say things out loud without thinking. After bending down to get the washing out of the machine, I said "oh my back's killing me" and Hope ran off in floods of tears, screaming that I was dying. It took me a good twenty five minutes to calm her down.

Social media has been a godsend for me. I don't have the time to maintain more than three fully functional friendships and even then, I only get together with my closest friends, about once every two to three months. Social media, means that I can keep track of what a wider circle of acquaintances are doing, when I have the odd couple of seconds to check my news feed and maybe add a like or comment, to show that I still care. Unfortunately, the kids seem to use the opportunity of me being on the PC as their chance to attack each other, so my online conversations, can take whole days, with me just tapping a response now and again, when I get a precious couple of free seconds. I think they do it on purpose, so that I'll move away from the computer and then they can jump on.

Whilst they were at school, I managed to get some peaceful online time and I think I may have finally found my new hobby. After careful consideration, I concluded that I might have been a little too quick to dismiss the idea of attending a weekly class. After all, if I'm happier, then surely the kids won't begrudge me an hour a night, once a week and if they have a happy Mum, then hopefully they'd be happier too. To be honest, as long as John keeps the drinks and snacks coming, I doubt if they'll even look up from their tablets to realise that I'm not even there.

I just need to be able to talk about something that isn't child or special needs related for half an hour a week. After scouring the internet, I found that there's a dance school nearby that is giving free taster classes every night, for one week only. I cast my eyes down the various list of classes. 'Tap' (no that would give me a headache.) 'Jazz' (I don't think so.) 'Hip Hop' (I think I'm nearer to a hip op!) There was only one other choice, so I went for it … 'Burlesque!'

As a kid, I grew up watching old Gene Kelly and Fred Astaire type films and I loved all that old time, Hollywood glamour. The women were so sexy back then, they had boobs and hips and were positively festooned with feathers and headdresses. In my head, one taster session of forty five minutes, was going to transform me, into a glamorous old time movie siren (and not the duffle coated, four foot nothing, frumpy mum that I'd go in as.)

At six o'clock prompt, I found myself sat in a room full of strangers, wondering whether I was doing the right thing and counting how many steps were between me and the door, in case I needed to make a quick exit.

The room had a sign hanging above the door, which read 'The Boudoir.' The lighting was provided by table lamps with corset style shades and colourful swathes of chiffon were draped over vintage, full length mirrors. The seat, I sat on was a wooden chair with a small round back that had been painted gold. A little part of me, wanted to grab it with one hand, flip it around, sit on it with one leg either side (even though my legs would be too short to touch the floor) and burst into song. In reality, I sat there with my arms crossed, checking out the other women.

Luckily the group was mixed, as far as sizes and ages went and to my delight, I realised that I didn't feel too self-conscious about my age or weight. In fact, nearly everyone else looked as nervous as me. There were a couple of women aged around the fifty mark, who had obviously come together, for moral support. There was a very ample young girl, who looked to be in her mid-twenties. An amazon of a girl, who was possibly still young enough to be called a teenager and had added to her already impressive height, by wearing sky scraper heels and looked like a beauty queen. Two best friends, who looked about my age were whispering quietly and lastly, was a woman that could have been anywhere between twenty eight and forty eight. She was dressed head to toe, in vintage fifties clothing and seemed far more assured than any of the other women sat in the circle, facing one another.

I thought Burlesque would be a good idea for me, because it's one of the few occasions I've found, where it's actually a benefit if you have ample curves. With Burlesque, there's much more freedom to be creative and it's all about the tease, rather than the striptease, unlike pole dancing, which is actually called that because most of the girls are about the same width as the pole and when they stand behind it, they actually disappear. (This may not be an actual proven fact and I may just be a tiny bit jealous!)

The instructor 'Fifi Firecracker,' (I'm not totally convinced that this is her real name) was everything I expected. Dark red hair was brushed into long waves, cascading around her shoulders, which perfectly matched the crimson lip gloss she wore, positively oozing vintage glamour. Her impressively perky cleavage, was held in check by a tight blouse and a black pencil skirt and patent stilettos, finished the outfit. She was like Jessica Rabbit, come to life. After giving us a talk about the history of Burlesque, she had us sauntering about the place, while twirling a feather boa around on one finger, which we then threw over our shoulders, (I felt very naughty) then she had us practicing pin up poses, which was slightly nerve wracking. Trying to strike sexy poses in a room full of strangers, was like the most intimidating job interview ever. Especially, when you caught sight of yourself in a full length mirror, trying to emulate a forties pin up girl.

I'm not altogether sure if I was relieved or disappointed that we didn't do any tassel twirling, I've always thought I would be quite good at it. It must have gone well for everyone though, because at the end of the session, we all signed up for a month long course called 'Beginner's Burlesque.' I dread to think what the PTA mums would make of it, if they could have seen me swaying my hips. (Claudia Greenacre, would ban me from entering the school gates if she ever found out.)

I thought perhaps I might keep it to myself for a little while. It makes it more exciting to have a naughty secret, even though, I had initially wanted to find a hobby that I could actually talk to people about.

Chapter Seventeen - Help I'm Having A Breakdown

After dragging myself out of my cosy warm bed, I made and ate my breakfast, prepared the packed lunches and filled juice bottles, I ran upstairs to wake the kids and get them ready for school.

Hope ran past me into the bathroom and sitting hurriedly on the toilet, she said. "Mummy I couldn't get to the toilet in time and I think I wet my bed." It was the first time that this had ever happened and I didn't want to cause her any anxiety, so I brushed a stray hair from her face and forced a bright smile (trying not to think about how I really didn't have time to strip the bed down this morning.)

"It's OK sweetheart. It was just an accident." All the commotion, had woken Jamie from his slumber and as he wandered into the bathroom, Hope said "has Jamie ever wet the bed." In her innocent little question, I saw the chance to tackle something, that might come up in the future and if it did, I didn't want Jamie to panic and be embarrassed, so I said "no he hasn't, but at some point, as he gets older, he might."

Both children stopped and looked at me, with open curiosity. "It's just, that when a boy gets older, he might have a sexy dream and then stuff might come out the end of his willy while he's asleep, but if it does it's OK. Mummy will just wash the bedding and it's all OK." Smiling encouragingly, I looked at my children. Hope, had lost all interest, but Jamie was looking at me, with a frown on his face. He said nothing for about ten minutes, until we were downstairs and then he whispered. "That thing you were talking about earlier. Did you mean M A S T U R B A ?"

"No" I said, cutting him off. "I didn't mean that. Masturbating, means when you play with it."

"What ?" He was aghast. "Why on earth would you do that ?" Trying not to laugh, I looked at him as gravely as I could. "Some boys do, but that's not important. I just want you to know that, you need never be embarrassed to talk about things. It's a natural part of being a boy." He let it go for several minutes and then muttered. "I'll never have dreams like that. That sort of thing won't happen in our house."

What with the bed stripping and the adolescent advice, I was seriously running behind time, getting the kids ready for school and nursery. Unable to even put my make up on, I managed to get them dressed and breakfasted in double quick time, threw their bags into the car and frantically hustled them (which isn't easy when they're both absorbed in their tablets) into our big blue estate and sped away, desperately hoping that there wouldn't be too much traffic along our fourteen mile journey. I was just making up time, when I looked down and to my horror, noticed that the airbag warning light was shining in all its bright orangeyness.

With a deep sigh, I pulled over into a narrow lay-by adjoining a local rugby club and started turning the engine on and off repeatedly, but the light remained stubbornly on. Jamie didn't really help, he kept saying "how long are we going to be here ? What's happening ? Are we going to be late ? Is it safe to park here ? When are we going to be going again ?"

I rang John at work (who is after all a mechanic) and he told me to ring the breakdown recovery service! (Seriously what is the point in having a mechanic for a husband, if he's not going to help, when you've broken down ?)

After one phone call on my mobile that cost me all of five pounds sixty, the breakdown people said we were being classed as a priority and they would be with us within an hour… an hour and that's with priority!!!

As I sat there in the car, (which was becoming colder by the minute,) with two children who were starting to get slightly restless, I looked up from my phone to find out that I had been blocked in by two scaffolding lorries the occupants of which, had gone to visit the food wagon across the road. Terrified that the breakdown recovery service wouldn't be able to find us, I swivelled in my seat trying to locate the offenders, when Jamie said "we will be at school at eight thirty two won't we ? I always get out of the car at exactly eight thirty two." Before I could tell him through gritted teeth, that we would get there when we get there and that I wasn't sat in a freezing cold lay-by, for fun, Hope said the four worst words I could possibly hear at that moment. "I need a wee."

This was the point at which I burst into tears. I was miles from a toilet (thank you council cutbacks), stuck in a car that I couldn't drive and Jamie was getting more anxious as the clock inched its way nearer to eight thirty two. In utter desperation I rang John to see if he could come and get Hope and take her to find a toilet. He said "no." I shouted at him something along the lines of "what is the point of being married to you ?" Before he could answer, I ended the call and cried all over again. As the temperature continued to drop, a nice man called back from the breakdown service to say that there was nothing they would be able to do. They said I should drive the car and just take it to the nearest dealer, as soon as possible. Luckily, the scaffolders had moved whilst I was on the phone and I spent the rest of the drive to the nearby public toilets, trying not to cross my hands over the wheel, in case the airbag flew out and broke my nose.

Once Hope had relieved herself, we sped along the roads to school, I couldn't hear the radio, because I had Jamie in the background, constantly asking "is it eight thirty two yet ? How long is it going to be ? Are we going to be late ?"

Luckily, I managed to get Jamie to school before they took the register. The downside was, I had to spend the rest of the morning sat in the garage, bored out of my mind whilst my car got fixed. Just in time, for me to turn around and go and do the school and nursery run again.

Being a little later than normal this morning, had obviously had an effect on Jamie for the rest of the day. When I went to collect him, his teacher told me that he had been unsettled and shouty all day. (Jamie, not the teacher.) Apparently, he had even been made to sit by himself on a table facing a wall, so he wouldn't get distracted.

Without giving me a chance to respond, Mr Rawlings stepped aside and introduced me to a red haired, voluptuous woman who I hadn't even noticed, standing slightly behind him. The beaming lady was the new school Educational Psychologist, who shook my hand rather too enthusiastically and said "I'm Gemma Anstey. Pleased to meet you."

Ms Anstey motioned to Mr Rawlings that his participation was not required and returned her wide smile in my direction. "I've just been observing Jamie this afternoon" she said, as I held my breath and waited for her to list a catalogue of reasons why he couldn't continue at the school. "He's a very clever little boy" she smiled, as I noisily exhaled in relief. "You'll get my report in a couple of weeks' time. But, I just had to tell you, I asked Jamie what he wanted to be when he grew up. Now at this age, we normally get answers like a spaceman, a footballer or a rock star. Jamie however, said he wanted to have his own logistics company called 'Jaylink' that worked out of European ports. To be honest, I have no doubt that he'll do it. However, he might want to think about Oxford University as a backup. He really would make a fantastic science or maths professor."

I stood stunned, watching Ms Anstey as she sashayed her way across the playground in her chunky heeled court shoes and tweed skirts and I kissed my clever little boy on the head, as he stood nervously waiting with John. "Oxford University as a backup." I laughed, as we walked towards the car. "Our boy's a flipping genius." I shouted, embarrassing Jamie, as I went.

When we arrived home, the thrill of the promise of Jamie's future, still bathed me in a warm fuzzy glow, but as I heard Jamie switch the TV on and then start screaming, I was brought back down to earth with a bump.

Jamie's fear of the new Alton Towers TV advert is really getting out of hand. It shows a guy whose eyes spin around, as they turn a green and black colour. It's got to the point where he's so terrified of seeing it, that if I watch a programme that has adverts, I have to quickly turn over onto BBC, so that the Alton Towers advert won't surprise him, by suddenly appearing before him on a forty eight inch screen. Sometimes, I buy pizzas or cereal that are sponsored by Alton Towers and he makes me cut the picture off of the box and throw it in the bin, before I'm allowed to have the boxes in the kitchen. Jamie had turned the TV on and before he could turn it over to a safe channel, the dreaded advert had suddenly appeared on the screen and he spent ten minutes hiding in his room, until I could assure him that it was safe to come down again. I really can't wait for them to have a new ride to publicise.

Following a night of advert free TV, the kids were finally settled in bed and I was just beginning to relax when Jamie whispered to Hope that she wasn't going to get any pocket money because she'd been a naughty girl. Hope got so angry, that she kicked Jamie right in his sensitive area and he fell off the bed howling in agony.

Now, he did start it, but she shouldn't have retaliated like that. I settled Jamie down, but he was still red in the face and teary and then I pulled Hope out from the bottom of the bed, where she was trying to hide unobserved under the duvet. "Hope. You need to say sorry to Jamie." My words had turned Hope's face as red as her brother's and she was crying just as hard. When she gets like that, I usually give in and end up apologising to her! I was determined not to cave in. "Hope. Say sorry to Jamie."

Defiantly, she shook her head and crossed her chubby little arms tightly against her chest. "If you don't say sorry, you'll have to go in your own room, until you're ready to say it." I have NEVER left her alone in her bedroom before, even when she was a baby, so I was really hoping that Hope wouldn't call my bluff and make me into the bad mum… She did!

The look of shock on her face was awful, as I left her standing in the doorway of her room. We don't have a landing at the top of our stairs and our bedroom doorframe actually touches Hope's, it wasn't as though I had left her alone in the east wing or anything, but from her reaction you would have thought I had.

Every three minutes I would go into her room and try to get her to say the 's' word, but she wouldn't (or to be honest it was more like she couldn't.) John and I played 'good cop, bad cop' and each time I walked out of her room, I was determined not to go back in, but I just couldn't stand the torture of her tears and really wanted the whole thing resolved. I tried every angle I could think of to cajole or threaten her, but underneath the mass of snot and tears, was a hardened core. Had my daughter been a spy in the Second World War, the Nazis would never have broken her.

In the end, I got her to speak by saying "Hope. Say snake," when she did, I got her to say 'sausages,' she was giggling by this time, so I snuck in "say sorry" and really quietly she said it. I gave her a big hug, told her that she was a good girl and let her come back into our bed.

I hate it when I have to be strong, when all I actually want to do is give her a hug and make it all better. Still, at least it only took an hour for her to apologise.

Chapter Eighteen - Hen Don't

I needed to take Jamie to the opticians to see if they can do anything about his new glasses that keep rubbing against his ears and causing him immense pain. I thought it was him being over sensitive at first, but it actually caused an open sore, on the top of his ear.

11.00 am. I managed to coax Jamie into coming up to the bedroom and then asked him to get dressed. I laid his clothes out for him, hoping that it would make it easier for him to try and get ready.

11. 01am. Forced to explain (once again,) where we were going and why I needed him to get dressed.

11.03 am. Had to help Jamie with his jeans, because he couldn't get them off the hanger or undo the buttons.

11.06 am. Asked Jamie to put his socks on.

11.10 am. Had to ask him to put his socks on again.

11.13 am. Jamie made me explain why he had to wear socks and why he couldn't wear crocs. Told him that because it was raining, I wanted him to wear proper shoes with socks and not sandals.

11.18am. He was still moaning about the socks and trying to work out exactly how many seconds he would be out of doors for and how long it would take to get to and from the car etc and if I was right in my assumption that he would get wet, or whether he could chance it in crocs.

11.24am. I'm sorry to say but after 24 minutes of trying to get Jamie dressed and ready, I lost my rag and shouted at him to "just put the bloody socks on and stop arguing for once in your life." It wasn't my proudest parenting moment, but the constant pressure and need to justify everything, often gives me a headache.

It took me ten minutes to drive to the opticians and precisely five minutes for the optician to adjust them. All in all, it took longer to get him ready, than the actual appointment lasted. Story of my life!

The stress of the morning's events were forgotten, by the time that the sky began to darken, as the watery sun, gave up its attempts at providing any warmth. It was time to get ready for the hen do I had been invited on. It was my first hen do in fifteen years. (I didn't even have one myself, when John and I got married.)

My friend Rose, is marrying her best friend and he really is a wonderful man. I have known her since we were both fifteen and I couldn't be happier for her. The hen do was going to be awesome!

I curled my hair for the first time in… ever and put on my rainbow coloured false nails and long thick black eyelashes. I really went for it. I don't get much chance to dress up, so I was excited. Rose and her husband to be, picked me up at seven thirty and after kissing the kids (and John of course) goodbye, I headed out into the night.

Meeting with the other girls (all of whom were mothers and girlfriends or wives) was exciting. We had a lovely meal in a little Italian restaurant and I spent most of the meal, talking to Rose's mum about kids and mortgage rates etcetera. It was all very grown up and sophisticated.

Some of the lightweights left at the end of the meal, whilst the rest of us hardcore girls, powered on through to the eighties club at the end of the road.

It felt so weird going into a nightclub for the first time in over a decade and a half. I must admit I felt a bit lost without John there and I missed the kids something terrible, but I tried to put those feelings aside and concentrated on the bride to be. We were seated in a red fake leather booth (which was supposed to be luxurious, but was actually covered in cigarette burns and patched in places) and all had a couple of flutes of something bubbly and then it was time to dance.

Rose's dark blonde hair fell in waves around her shoulders and she positively glowed with happiness, as she danced in her pink sash, which proclaimed that she was soon to be a bride. There was a really good atmosphere amongst our group, because everyone there was already in a happy relationship and no one was trying to find a man, so we all stuck together and had a good time. Whenever a drunken bloke came over to one of us, the others would close ranks and squeeze him out, it was harsh, but reassuring for an old married woman like me.

We had a great night and at one am (five hours past my normal bedtime) it was time for us to go. Rose's fiancé was waiting outside to give us a lift home bless him and we left the coloured lights, the smoke machine, the music and the drunks lying in the gutter and headed home.

I put the key quietly in the door and crept softly up the stairs. John would be getting up for work shortly, so I was acting like a ninja, trying not to wake anyone. Pushing the bedroom door open, I found the TV on and John sitting up in bed with Hope awake next to him. "What's going on ?" I whispered, confused about the welcome party. Both heads swivelled to look at me and then Hope said in her sternest voice. "I wouldn't go to sleep because you weren't here!"

It seems like my first hen do in fifteen years, would be my last. It might take another fifteen years for Hope to forgive me, for being a bad mother, who's ready to abandon her children at a mere decade and a half's notice.

Chapter Nineteen - Exits Are ALWAYS Through The Gift Shop

I didn't really have much to drink at the hen do, but I felt hung over none the less due to the lack of sleep. Because of Hope's comments about me going out, I felt like the world's worst mother, so thought I'd make it up to the kids by taking them somewhere nice. There's an aeroplane museum on an RAF Base that I used to go to when I was in school and I thought the kids might like it. Also, with the weather being horrendous, our entertainment options were fairly limited.

11.00am. Arrived at the aeroplane museum (the same one that I had been trying to get Jamie to go to for three years and somehow was now deemed acceptable by him.) It said on the poster to allow four and a half hours to look around all the exhibits.

11.05 am. Hope started asking if she could go and look in the shop, but we managed to distract her with some crayons and a picture of a plane to colour in. Jamie wandered around looking bored. It felt like it was unofficial Asperger's Museum Visit Day, as all the kids were about Jamie's age. The place was filled with young boffin types, talking loudly about all the components needed to make a jet engine, or maximum thrust (It was immensely entertaining.)

11.15 am. Hope announced that she had finished looking at the 'boring' planes and wanted to go to the shop.

11.20am. Walked into an interactive part of the museum, that had no warnings before the entrance, on what lay behind so we just assumed that 'interactive' meant buttons you could press or costumes you could put on.

We opened the door and stepped into a dark hangar, where all the planes were in darkness and a booming voice announced that a helicopter was about to land. The flaps at the back of a jet start moving, smoke came out, lights went off and there was a deafening roar, as the voice announced that the jet was going to take off. Well you can imagine how well that went down! Jamie thought the planes were actually going to move and Hope was distraught at the loud noise, within seconds both of them were blindly running around, trying to find the exit, in a total panic.

11.26 am. In the shop! (So much for the four and a half hour experience.)

It was soul destroying really. You could see that there was nothing in particular that they wanted, but neither could they pass up the opportunity to buy something. John and I kept passing one another, as we followed a child around (one of our children of course,) in the end we were giving ultimatums and counting down how long they had left before we walked out of the building, with or without a purchase. After twenty minutes, they bought two little metal planes, which cost the same as buying two real life size ones. We had spent forty five minutes inside the building and almost half of it had been spent inside the shop.

Chapter Twenty - A Right Pain In The Balls

One morning, I found, I was able to snatch five minutes for a cup of coffee, whilst Hope was watching one of the children's channels. In between the programmes, the annoyingly buoyant presenters are normally doing something inane, but this time, I couldn't believe it when one of them said "let's play a game. It's called ten things you can do with a banana." (Now, it might be my own warped mind) but I spat my coffee out, straight across the floor, narrowly missing a confused Hope's head!!!

When John returned home from work, I popped to the local supermarket, because apparently it was too cold for my little sensitive darlings to venture outdoors. Jamie had asked for a certain variety pack of crisps for his packed lunch and I had been duly dispatched to get them. I scoured the aisles of Tesco, but they only had an empty space where the crisps Jamie wanted, should have been. Knowing, that I didn't dare go home without them, I drove three miles to Sainsbury's and once again, I was out of luck. Feeling that I had done enough to fulfil his wishes, I rang the home phone. John answered "can I speak to Jamie please ?" I knew I was quite short with him, but I was on my mobile and time was literally money.

There was silence, as the phone was passed over and I heard John say "it's Mummy, say hello." I was just able to pick out the quiet, squeak of "hello" and so I said, "Jamie, its Mummy. I've tried two supermarkets and I can't find the crisps you asked for. Is there anything else I could get ?".... Nothing, just silence, I couldn't even hear him breathing. "Hello... Hello ?" Finally, I heard John pick up the phone again. "What's going on ?" He asked.

"I asked Jamie a question and was waiting for an answer. Why what's he doing ?" My husband sounded really irritated now. "I came back in from the kitchen, the phone was dangling on its cord and Jamie is back on the internet. He must have just dropped the phone and walked away."

I laughed, because I knew I couldn't even be surprised. Jamie doesn't like talking to people face to face, let alone when they're on the other end of a phone. "What did you ask him ?" John, was less accepting of Jamie's little quirks than I was.

"I just wanted to know if there were any other crisps I could get him." I heard him shouting my question at Jamie, then I heard an angry voice yell back. "There is nothing else that I want."

"Why didn't you answer Mummy, when she asked you ?"

"Because she should already know." Saving my breath, my battery, my phone credit and my sanity, I just said "OK" and drove home, to my sulky and disappointed son, who would never appreciate the efforts I go to, for him.

Even at midnight, I am still on duty. Jamie found his way back into our bed and I really didn't have the energy to settle him back down in his own room, so, because there was no space for me in my own bed as Jamie tends to fidget, whilst sleeping in a starfish position, I had to concede defeat and went into his room to find some space to get my head down. Throwing his toys on the floor, I gratefully threw myself down onto his empty bed.

At one am, Hope came and found me asleep in Jamie's room. Not up for the fight of going into her room and sitting with her for forty minutes while she settled down, I just let her get into Jamie's bed with me. Unfortunately, Hope sleeps sideways and noisily sucks her thumb so I couldn't get much sleep anyway.

Woke up at two am, because I was getting kicked in the face by two tiny little feet, which had a surprising amount of force behind them. Five minutes later, Jamie walked into his room looking for me. Whilst he settled down to sleep, I crept out, leaving the children sleeping soundly and crept silently back into my own bed.

At four am John's alarm went off for him to get up for work.

Six am and the alarm went off again for me. How could I still feel tired, even though I'd only just woken up ?

I had Jamie's annual statement review at two thirty and could have done with a good night's sleep, in order to be alert. I know we're all there for the same purpose and we're all supposed to be on the same side, but I do feel a bit defensive and a bit like I'm being ganged up on sometimes. I suppose it's because, to the professionals, he is one boy out of many, who has a problem that they have to deal with and for me, he's my beautiful, clever and vulnerable son, who struggles with the daily restrictions that they place upon him. You never can tell how the meeting is going to go beforehand, but thankfully, it seemed to go very well.

As he is in Year 4 now, they will continue to keep up his one to one support as the work will be more challenging for him as he nears his SATS year. The problem that Jamie seems to have, is that he is fantastic at maths, reading and science, but anything creative where he has to use his imagination, he just cannot do it and has a meltdown. Came away from the meeting in a positive frame of mind, which doesn't always happen.

Luckily the meeting had been scheduled for the end of the day and I was just on my way to go and stand outside Jamie's classroom, when the deputy head stopped me and in lowered tones said. "Can you go and have a word with Mr Rawlings ?" I was instantly on the alert. Anytime the deputy or even worse the Headmistress, stops to tell you to have a word with your child's teacher the alarm bells go blaring. "Why does Mr Rawlings want to see me ?"
He leaned in closer and said "He's hurt his testicles." This conversation was so surreal, I started to think that perhaps I was actually dreaming. "I mean Jamie's had a pain in his testicles obviously, not Mr Rawlings." He clarified. Seeing his flustered expression (I'm embarrassed to admit) I actually snorted out loud.

"Well" I laughed "that would have been one awkward conversation. Glad you cleared that up."

As the deputy hurried away, looking as red as a tomato. I started to worry about poor Jamie and his painful testicles. Mr Rawlings came out at the end of the day and said "Jamie had a pain in his testicles today." I could see that he thought I was a totally heartless bitch, as I stood in front of him, desperately trying to stop another fit of giggles. Shouldering his way between us, Jamie shouted "I'm fine! Can everyone please stop talking about my balls in the playground please ?"

Driving home from school was a subdued affair until Jamie suddenly said "Mummy the connectivity part of my mobile phone doesn't work anymore. It's OK though, I'm going to put in under my pillow tonight and then I'll get money from the Bluetooth Fairy." It's the first time he's ever made up a joke, I was so proud of him. I kept chuckling all the way home.

My children are a teensy bit needy and secretly I love that they want to be with me all of the time (even though in front of other people, I feel forced to agree to statements from other mums, when they say things like "oh yes, it's very important that children should be independent from as young an age as possible.") On the hand it does get a little bit draining, when I can't even go to the toilet on my own. I really wanted a nice warm, hot bath and so I tried my usual tactic and crept up the stairs, whilst Hope and Jamie were watching a kid's TV programme with John. As I sank down into the hot water with a book and began to relax, I heard a chilling question. "Mummy, are you upstairs or downstairs ?" Next, I heard the ominous sound of footsteps stomping up the stairs and then Hope's little face appeared over the top of the bath.

The first thing she said was "are you getting out now ?" She stood there and watched me rub the shampoo into my hair with an evil gleam in her eye and then, as I lay back in the water with my eyes closed (rookie mistake) and began to rinse the shampoo out, it happened! She chucked a jug of water over my face, trying to help me (so she claimed) with the rinsing process.

I didn't see it coming. I just felt a burning pain as the water filled my nose and the back of my throat and I struggled to breathe and I fought against the panic of drowning. Opening my eyes, I saw Hope smiling at me, waiting for praise for all her helpfulness, at my lovely clean hair. So much for a relaxing bath. I'd have to ensure that I had showers whilst Hope still harboured homicidal tendencies. I didn't have time to dwell on my near death experience. I had a Burlesque class to get to.

I felt a frisson of excitement as I walked through the doors into the boudoir room. Still overwhelmed with feelings of guilt at going out for an hour and leaving John with the kids (especially the little scary one,) I took a deep breath and stepped into the airy dance space.

Dressed up in my fifties tea dress, wearing my brightest scarlet lipstick, I was feeling authentic and ready to have fun. I had just spent the last hour, trying to coax my stubborn hair into victory rolls, before finding out that they are almost impossible to create with freshly washed locks. I had so many products on my hair by the time I got to class, I had to be careful to stay away from any naked flames.

Before I left, I had stupidly asked Jamie. "How do I look ?" After giving me the once over, he seemed to make his decision and then said. "Well, I think you were going for fifties glamour, but you've achieved a cheap eighties knock off look" !!!!!!!! That's the last time I ever ask his opinion... on ANYTHING.

All the other girls were already there and as I walked towards my seat, they all turned to smile at me. I noticed that without exception, every one of them were dressed in jeans and plain sweatshirts and wore no make-up at all. I couldn't help but feel a bit slutty in seamed suspenders, underneath a tight fitting, high waisted skirt, but I tried to assume a Katy Perry style outer confidence, as I held my head high and found my seat.

Luckily the girls didn't hold my efforts against me and we were soon put into groups, practising a routine which involved dragging chairs around (I loved that bit the best.)

Towards the end, we placed our chairs in a circle and Fifi asked us what our aspirations were for the course. Some people said that they'd always wanted to do Burlesque but had always been too scared. Some said that they wanted more self-confidence and to feel happy with who they are. When it came to my turn, I said "I just wanted to have a hobby. Something exciting. Something I could talk to my husband about."

All things considered, it was a blissful hour and was over before I even realised it. When I got home, I actually had something of my own to talk about and funnily enough, John didn't seem to mind, talking about anything that involved removing clothes.

As I lay there in bed, I realised that I had introduced myself at the class, as 'Sarah.' Not Hope's mum, not Jamie's mum and not John's wife, in fact I never even had a chance to give any witty anecdotes about the children. It was the one place that I have been in the last nine years, where people just knew me as Sarah and that was both a weird and cool feeling at the same time. There was still a small feeling of guilt, but overall I wish I'd done it years ago.

Chapter Twenty One - On The History Trail

I finally achieved a lifelong ambition, taking the kids to see Hampton Court Palace. To them, it meant a journey spent eating sweets, playing games on the DS and watching DVDs. Followed by looking around a beautiful palace, eating a fun picnic and then buying their heart's desire in the shop, before being chauffeured home again, with their evening meal cooked and placed before them, whilst they relaxed in front of the TV.

For John and I (but mostly I) it meant, booking the tickets in advance, making sure I printed the confirmation and taking note of the postcode for the Satnav. Getting up at five thirty in the morning, in order to give myself time to get dressed and then single handedly preparing a picnic for four people, using ingredients, I had picked up from the supermarket the day before. Then there was the three hour drive, trying to fight through the horrendous Bracknell traffic and worrying about where to park and if I have enough change to pay for it. Then we spend the time, shepherding the children around the palace, ensuring that they don't break anything or cross any red velvet ropes, before letting them go into the gift shop, where they spend a small fortune on things they'll forget about in three days' time. Then, I have the arduous task of driving all the way home again, before cooking the kid's tea, clearing everything away after and then running the children a bath. Even just thinking about it, makes me tired.

They had one of those trail things, where you have to look for things dotted around the building and grounds. I HATE THOSE TRAILS. They stop me from absorbing the atmosphere of the palace and Jamie gets really upset if he can't find or work out all of the clues. I can't imagine Henry the Eighth walking around, if I'm busy trying to spot a phoenix on the ceiling or a swan in a tapestry.

We managed to get out of the shop within ten minutes, as they both decided on a red and gold tunic each, with matching swords and happily fought, all the way to the car.

As we pulled out of the car park, Jamie said "can we go to Warwick Castle tomorrow ?" Despite not wanting to spend another day behind the wheel, I can never resist a castle, so I ended up agreeing to go, but did warn them that we wouldn't be spending much money in the shop at Warwick. They both reluctantly agreed, so hopefully talking to them like adults and making them understand that you can't have everything you want in life, has finally got through to them.

A few weeks ago, Jamie decided that we should have a Saturday night takeaway for our evening meal. As he is the most unadventurous child ever, I wanted to encourage any interest on his part towards new foods and experiences and so John and I agreed.

As we neared our house, we saw a sign on the window, stating that our local Chinese takeaway would be closed for two weeks. John said he would drive to the next nearest shop, but Jamie refused point blank to have any food from there and made me cook him a chicken fillet from the freezer at home.

Hope decided that she wanted to go with John to get the food and off they went. She is always up for a new adventure. Once we were alone, Jamie confided that the reason he was so angry and wouldn't have any food, was because it wasn't from the usual place and he was nervous of trying something new.

When they came back, Hope was proudly brandishing a fortune cookie that she had been given by the lady in the shop, who had been taken in by her impish charm. Jamie circled the food like a vulture and then declared that next time, he would be the one that went to the shop with John and check out whether it was sufficient to provide him with food. Honestly, even getting a takeaway is hard work.

Chapter Twenty Two - On The Road Again

At eight am, we left for Warwick Castle. The kids were sat in the back with a fully charged DS and tablet each and a DVD screen each, to watch their choice of a huge array of DVDs. Yet, I know that at some point, they will still complain that being in the car is boring!!! Despite all the technology they have, we end up playing 'I eye spy something coloured' (because Hope doesn't know what letter things start with.) The only problem with playing this game, is that Hope thinks of random things she has seen, heard about or even imagined at some point in her life and not something that her eye can actually spy at that exact moment, when she's playing the game!

At nine am, the 'are we there yets ?' started. At nine forty five, we got to the castle just before it opened and even managed to park in the tarmaced car park and not the overflow field miles away. Result! (It's generally a bad day, when the kids are tired of walking, BEFORE we even get to the castle itself.) Jamie got really upset at ten am, because we stopped to watch the raising of the portcullis. This amazing entertainer sets the mood and tells you all about the history and function of the portcullis, but Jamie kept complaining loudly that they should just open it and not give a lecture and kept asking when it was going to go up. When the guy got the crowd to shout "A Warwick, A Warwick." Jamie started shouting, "A Boring, A Boring." The portcullis went up and the crowd cheered, and Jamie moaned all the way up through the gateway and into the courtyard, luckily we were in a tight press of people and I could pretend I wasn't with him.

Jamie decided that he wasn't going to do the dungeons, the dragon tower, the waxwork exhibitions, the bird of prey talk, the ramparts or the Victorian school experience (which didn't leave much.) So we went to watch the jousting.

One of Jamie's problems, is that he can never tell when he needs to use the toilet. We know he needs the loo, because we see him jiggling around, but because he doesn't pick up on the signals, he gets embarrassed and angry that we know something he doesn't and he fights us all the way. Jamie had started jiggling, so John took him to the toilet, even though Jamie was insistent he didn't need to go. Jamie refuses to use the urinals in a public toilet, so John took him into the cubicle. When they had finished (and surprise, surprise, Jamie had actually used the bathroom) John came marching out with a face like thunder. "That is the last time I ever take him to the toilet" he said. I looked at both their faces and wondered what disaster could have befallen them in the last four minutes. "What happened ?" I asked and lowering his voice, John recounted the story, whilst Jamie stood behind him glowering in anger.

Apparently, John had bundled Jamie into the toilet, whilst Jamie started shouting "don't make me do it Daddy. Please don't make me get my willy out. I don't want to do it." John's face was completely red, by the time he finished and Jamie was completed unrepentant. "I didn't think I needed to go." I tried really hard not to laugh at John's indignant face. "Luckily" he said "there wasn't anyone else in there, but I am never taking him again. Someone could get the wrong idea and a quick toilet break, could land me in prison."

At eleven thirty precisely, I took Hope to the Princess Tower which was really magical. She had her photo taken and sat with the other little girls throughout the whole thing, which was a big deal for her and I stood with the other parents, ever the proud Mummy. As soon as we were finished, we ran to the river to meet with Jamie and John who were watching the Fireball Trebuchet.

Hope and I got there just in time to see the giant trebuchet fire a flaming ball through the air and onto the grass. It was really exciting, but Jamie was claiming to be bored, so we went to get some food, hoping that would cheer him up.

At one o'clock, the picnic had been eaten and the children were in the shop. Hope picked out a fluffy pink dragon in the shop, so I agreed she could have it. Jamie asked what his budget was and I said "you have ten pounds." As usual, he got really annoyed because he'd spotted a Lego set for nineteen pounds. I pointed out that twenty was double his budget and he pointed out that it was nineteen pounds and not twenty pounds. (He really can't cope with rounding up.)

After some tears and storming about (half mine, half his,) I realised that if I said no to this one thing, Jamie would just remember the disappointment of when we left and the whole day would have been for nothing. So I bought the set. (God I despise my own weakness at times.)

1.20 pm. Got back to the car and told Jamie "under no circumstances do you open the Lego before we get home, because you'll lose the pieces."

1.25 pm. Jamie opened the bag and started trying to make up his set!!!!!!!!!

1.30 pm. Stopped shouting at Jamie about how he won't listen to anything I say.

1.35 pm. Jamie continued with the Lego building.

1.36 pm. We decided on saving our breath and ignoring him. If he lost any pieces, it would be his own fault.

One day, I promised to myself, we would spend a full day at an attraction.

Chapter Twenty Three - Starting A Dialogue

I am sooooooo tired!!! The kids were up and down ALL NIGHT.

I finally managed to go back to sleep at twenty past six in the morning, but I'd set the alarm for six forty, so by seven am, I was downstairs drinking coffee, whilst feeling like I was being stabbed in the eyes with a fork.

Once the kids had safely been deposited at school and nursery, I walked back into the living room, with my arms full of clean washing. I happened to catch a phone in on morning TV, a lady had called in to ask 'how do we tell our child that he has an Autism diagnosis ?' My sympathies are with anyone in that position and it made me think of how we broached the subject with Jamie for the first time.

Whenever we took him to see the Paediatrician, he would ask why he was going and we would tell him that, because he was so clever the Doctor wanted to meet him (which was true.) Finally, when he got his diagnosis, they recommended that we get a DVD that had been designed to help children with Asperger's to understand emotions. Jamie picked up the box and asked me what Asperger's Syndrome was. Not expecting to have the conversation so early and thinking on my feet I said. "People with Asperger's find it hard to talk to other people sometimes. They're extremely clever and sometimes they can get quite frustrated and angry." He went quiet for a moment, as I held my breath, watching him, trying to weigh up his possible reaction. He just looked at me and said. "That's me. I'm an Asperger."

Minutes later and he was online, ordering himself autistic aids, likes fiddle toys and bendy men. He also ordered some books aimed at children with Asperger's. The only things he has ever said about his diagnosis, was "oh so that's why I can't run as fast as some people" or "Asperger's is a select club of Super Heroes" and "Ignorant people think I've got a disability, but actually I've got a super ability and they should look at what I can do, not what I can't do."

Every child is different and it's hard to know when it's the right time to bring it up, but personally, I didn't want the Asperger's to feel like a dirty secret that he should be ashamed of. Jamie made it easy and we were really lucky. I tell everyone about his diagnosis and we always talk about it in a positive light. As soon as Hope was diagnosed we said, "You've got Asperger's" and she said
"Oh good, I'm like Jamie" so it wasn't a big deal for her either. Jamie's favourite saying, when he's done something silly is "I've been putting the ass into Asperger's since 2005."

I finished folding the washing and realised, we were at that time of year, when behaviour management, gets a whole lot easier. In our house, we have motion detectors in every room that give off a red light whenever anyone walks into its field of vision. When Jamie was three, I told him that the light goes off, whenever Santa is listening in, because he's trying to see who should be on the naughty or nice list. He still believes it now. If he's kicking off, all I have to do is look at the monitor and he instantly behaves. Another little white lie I told him was that I can't buy him any toys throughout October, November and December, because the elves have already started production by then and I don't want to anger them by going ahead and buying him something that they are already making.

Last year, he caught me hiding some toys for Hope in the boot of the car, so I explained that because of the recession, parents had been asked to help out by buying some of the presents and that Santa would send an elf down from the North Pole to collect them. I watched him closely, waiting to see if he would swallow this (given that he is so untrusting and switched on) he looked me squarely in the eyes and said very gravely "thank goodness for that. I thought you were going to tell me there was no Santa for a minute."

My problem is, I've done such a good job in convincing him that Santa exists, I'm frightened that when he's married with his own children, he won't realise that he has to buy them anything, because he's waiting for Santa to show up.

I always try to keep a positive attitude, but sometimes I do get overwhelmed by my children's conditions. I start to worry about Jamie especially and his future. Will he mature emotionally ? Will he manage his outbursts easier ? Will he have to become self-employed, because he'll forever be unable to work in a normal environment ? My biggest fear is that he will over react (which he is VERY prone to doing) and that he will do something stupid because he didn't get top marks in his exams or a girlfriend has split up with him. I try to stay calm and not go searching for trouble, but every now and again (especially when I'm tired) it's difficult. I try to remind myself, that he has made remarkable progress already, but time for reflection, is few and far between, when you feel like all you're doing is firefighting, disasters every day.

Hope's disability card arrived in the post, pulling me out of my nostalgic reverie. It's a little laminated card from the city council, which states she is on the local Disabled Children's Register. I take the card, (and a letter from the Paediatrician, explaining that the Asperger's diagnosis means that she has a problem with queuing,) along to big theme park type places and depending on where it is, we don't have to wait in long queues for attractions. The little card is also useful, because most attractions accept it as proof of disability and we get in free as carers or at a discount.

When I had been getting Hope's packed lunch ready for nursery, she asked me to make her a chocolate spread sandwich, shaped like the creeper from Minecraft!

She has totally the wrong idea when she plays Minecraft. Instead of building a block house and hiding from zombies and creepers (and if possible kill them,) but Hope likes them and actively goes out of her hiding place in the game to go and say hello to them.

I have no idea, why she thinks I have these wonderful, creative culinary skills, but as usual, I did my best to comply with her demands, whilst my creative director sat on the worktops bellowing orders at me. She seemed pleased enough with my efforts and when I picked her up from nursery the sandwich box was empty (unusual for her) so I must have done something right (unusual for me.)

When I was running his bath tonight, Jamie wandered into the bathroom and said, "I don't want it too hot. Remember I'm Autistic. I can feel fifty shades of heat." I laughed at his cheekiness, but made a mental note to hide my book collection in a more secure place.

3.00 am. Bloody marvellous! The one night where the kids haven't woken up yet and I'm still awake. My brain keeps going 'you should be awake at this time. What are you doing trying to sleep ?'

3.30 am. Just drifted off to sleep when I dreamt that there was a big spider on John's pillow and woke myself up,

4.00 am. Happily dozing, when John's alarm went off. I'm ashamed to say I swore at it and then at him.

5.00am. They say you learn something new every day and today, I found out that no matter how tired you are, it is impossible to sleep when you have a crazy little girl sitting on your legs, staring at you.

Despite, hitting a wall of tiredness at three pm. I was determined to make it to my Burlesque class. I had been looking forward to it all week. My actual friends at the school, I had confided in and they were really supportive, but as far as the judgemental mums knew, I was going to a dance class and that was that. It was great to have something to be excited about. The last time I had been so eagerly expectant, was when Jamie had been constipated. (Only a parent knows the feelings of anxiety and then elation when your child manages to have a bowel movement, after a prolonged period.)

It was the week that the class was focusing on corsets and suspenders and as I arrived, the sound of nervous laughter filled the air. Even the shyest women of the group, were clutching their corsets, stockings and suspender belts, ready to have a go. Fifi sashayed in, wearing a beautiful, crimson corset with matching retro suspender belt and luxurious seamed suspenders. (Clearly she hadn't bought the cheapest she could find, like we all had.)

Rushing off to the toilets, we all timidly, appeared in our suspenders, (albeit with hot pants or denim shorts under or over the belt.) I've had two children, so I'm not really bothered about being coy anymore. (When I was in hospital having Jamie, I was nearly at the point of asking anyone who passed the end of the bed, to check how dilated I was.) I simply wore a corset on top, but mostly everyone else, wore a t-shirt underneath theirs. (Trust me, to be the exhibitionist.) Once, everyone was in the same position, we all had a bit of a giggle and the last of the invisible walls between us evaporated, as we cast our inhibitions to the wind (or rather, our suspenders to the floor) and paraded around in our corsets.

It was quite liberating to see just how beautiful everyone looked, even though we were all very different shapes and sizes. There was a bit of suspender belt and corset envy going on I must say. Most of us had the usual thin, basic belts in a variety of colours, but two of the girls had these vintage black ones that were really deep and had three straps on each leg, instead of the usual two. I vowed to myself that the minute I got home, I would order one online. You can't act the part, if you don't look the part.

In my head, I didn't see myself as a middle aged mum in an empty room filled with mirrors. I saw myself sitting in a giant cocktail glass, as the star of a Vegas show. (Reality, really isn't my strong point sometimes.) Following my two caesarean sections, the only show I could star in, would be Embarrassing Bodies.

Chapter Twenty Four - Public Humiliation

As I drove to Jamie's school to watch his assembly, I started listening to a song on the radio today, written by a dad to his young daughter and trying to give her guidance on the world. Sadly, I don't think I stand a chance of protecting Hope from all the Casanovas and players of the world and that thought is terrifying. Even at the tender age of four years old, she definitely knows her own mind already. She is insistent that Darth Vader is a good guy and that everyone should be on the Dark side. Her favourite character in Wallace & Gromit is the penguin diamond thief. In Monsters Inc, her character of choice is the sly baddie, Randall. This doesn't particularly fill me with confidence about her choice of boyfriend, as she gets older. However, the other evening, we were watching a Michael Buble show, Hope took one look at him and said "ooh he's lovely." Stunned, I asked her

"Do you mean his voice or him ?" Without even thinking about it, she said

"I mean him." So perhaps she does have some taste after all.

Luckily I managed to find a parking space within a five mile radius of the school and went to find myself a seat in the hall. I absolutely hate seeing 'class assembly' on the school calendar and have been known to do a happy dance when an Eye Hospital appointment coincides with a much dreaded class assembly.

Every time this ritual nightmare rolls around, Jamie always asks for a speaking part and then gets scared during the actual performance, ending up with him just standing there, going red in the face. If the teacher has prior knowledge of Jamie's stage fright, they think they're being kind, by not giving him a part, he feels upset and insulted and then during the performance will get bored and start shuffling or walking about. I end up getting all hot because I know that all the other parents are looking at him and then, when it's all over, they come and tell me that they thought he was funny etcetera, or they give me a hug, if he's done particularly well and I honestly don't know which is worse, being pitied or patronised!

Unfortunately, it was a particularly terrible play (and I mean because of Jamie, not because of the other children who read too fast or two quietly and you don't know what the hell is going on.) He stood in the front of the class and then, as per usual, couldn't say his line. One of his little friends got up and stood beside him for support, but Jamie went all red in the face and sat down after a couple of minutes of total silence. AWFUL.

To compound the problem, he inveigled his way to the front and then whenever a child had to get up and say a line, they managed to kick Jamie on his leg, arm or at one point, even knocking his glasses off. It was torture, sitting there, watching him cry and being unable to go and cuddle him.

Finally, the nightmare was over and Jamie came walking towards me in floods of tears. He was getting himself all worked up and kept grabbing his head, saying it felt hot. I could see that he was heading for the mother of all meltdowns and I couldn't get him to calm down, because everyone was looking at him (children and parents.)

Earlier that morning, I had already taken his juice bottle down to the school, so I couldn't even offer him a cold drink. I did the only thing that I could think of, I persuaded his teacher to allow me to take him across the road, to the little village supermarket and get my son a cold drink. As the other kids walked back to school in the rain, I drove Jamie back in the car.

By the time the others arrived, he was changed out of his costume and feeling much happier (especially because he was the only one who was still warm and dry.) It may have been his worst class play to date, but I learned a valuable lesson about what warning signs he shows before a meltdown and how removing him from the situation worked wonders. I didn't realise how appropriate a word 'meltdown' is, when the person in question is physically overheating.

Luckily, later in the day, I had a Burlesque class to attend and I really needed a little bit of escapism and a reason to 'tart' myself up. Ms Firecracker swept into the room and announced that the first thing we needed to do, was choose our Burlesque names. We spent the first ten minutes throwing out the most ridiculous names, but in the end I went for 'Fifi La Belle,' whilst the girls around me, opted for more adventurous monikers.

Some girls were excited and couldn't wait to be the centre of attention (I was very firmly in this camp) and then there were the others who were a bit nervous, especially when Fifi Firecracker announced that we would be taking our corsets off and going down to pasties. After a lot of discussion, we all finally agreed that we were going to go for it. No sooner had we dealt with that, she also said she wanted us to start practising a group performance, which was yet another thing to get us excited and scared at the same time. I just managed to see my comfort zone, far away in the distance, as it slid out of view.

We started practising our routine, which was set to 'The Stripper.' The music automatically makes you sashay your hips as soon as it begins. My favourite part of the routine is when we drag the chair behind us with one hand and then flip it around quick in front of us, placing one stockinged, high heeled shoe on the seat. We might have been clumping about on a wooden floor in an old sugar factory, on a dark night, wedged into corsets, but in our heads we were Vegas showgirls. I could see it in the faces of the others too.

By the end of the night, the routine was coming along great. We were individually going through phases of exhilaration and doubt, all at different times, but we all rallied around and supported one another, which is the great thing about being part of a group. I left with the feeling that it could turn out to be something really special, I couldn't believe I was a part of it.

When I got home, it was time for one of the worst parts of the impending festive season. The time when school Christmas cards are exchanged. Jamie wrote his first card out, totally messed it up, got angry and threw it at me. So as usual, I ended up writing out thirty Christmas cards for his classmates (ably assisted by a glass of Merlot… or four,) whilst Jamie sorted through the pack, reserving the best cards for the friends he liked the most. To be honest, by the time I got to the last few, my handwriting was starting to resemble Jamie's, so at least his little friends would think it was him that had put in the effort.

When he was in his reception class at school. I took in a pack of Christmas cards that I'd written out and gave them to his lovely teacher, so that she could keep them in her desk and if everyone else got a card in the school post except him, then she could give him a card from Mummy and he would know he was loved. Thankfully, she never had to use any of them. (I think the wine's making me a little sentimental.)

Writing out so many greetings of the season, meant that I was up late ordering the grocery shopping online. It's much, much easier and far cheaper for me to do it that way. Also, you don't have to stand at the till whilst a judgemental cashier says things like, "oh he's a livewire" or the other classic, "hmm do you really need more sugar ?" You kind of don't want to make an issue out of it at first, and you smile politely, but after a while you want to shout at them for being so bloody rude.

I couldn't keep myself awake thinking of what annoyed me. I had to at least try and get some sleep before the first of my children woke up and the night shift began.

It really irritates me when a smug mum who has no idea of what it's like having children like mine says, "oh I need my sleep" or "I couldn't cope with my children, if they didn't sleep." As if I wake up several times in the night for a laugh, or because I think hey, sleep's overrated anyway, I love sleep deprivation. (Really thought the wine would have relaxed me. Grrrr.)

Chapter Twenty Five - Theatre Debut

I took Hope for her first ever visit to the theatre to see her beloved Peppa Pig live, whilst Jamie was at school. I seem to be doing a lot of things just with Hope, but Jamie is nine and we did so much more with him, when he was little. By the time he was four years of age, he had been to see lots of shows, (we had more money then, what with having one child and all.)

When he was the same age as Hope is now, we paid for a box for me, Jamie and John, to see the characters from The Tweenies in their own performance, because for that couple of months he had been really into them. Unfortunately, two days before the show, he came down with chickenpox, which spread over his face like a … well like a rash really. I didn't want him to miss the show, after he'd been so looking forward to going, plus it had cost fifty pounds for the tickets and John was livid about losing the money. In desperation, I sent my tight fisted husband out, to get any dress up costume with a full face mask that he could find.

Half an hour later, John came back with a red Power Rangers costume, we put the mask over Jamie's face outside the theatre and carried him into the lobby, where a woman checked our tickets. She looked at Jamie and said. "Hello. Who have we got under there ?" At this point, I felt like one of those drug smugglers you see on the TV getting anxious at border control. I was praying he wouldn't lift his mask up and luckily he didn't, but I nearly passed out, because I'd actually forgotten to breathe, whilst all this was going on. We sat in our box and Jamie got to enjoy the show, which made it all worth it. It's a story that Jamie still likes to tell and I try to shush him, because the adults smile politely at Jamie and then glare at me for my irresponsibility, but in my defence, we were in a box.

I'd actually bought the tickets for Hope and I to see Peppa Pig, fifteen months before the show. They had gone on sale last August and I thought the show was on in October of the same year, unfortunately, I didn't read it properly and it was for the following October. So poor Hope had to wait nearly a year and a half for her day out. Two weeks ago, she said she didn't want to go to the show and asked me to sell the tickets. Luckily, I know what she's like and although I agreed to sell them, I secretly didn't. I knew she would change her mind again the next day. It always pays to be one step ahead, where kids are concerned.

To be honest, I expected Hope to be more awed by the big theatre, but she just took it all in her stride. We were in the front row next to the aisle and luckily she approved of the seats. As the curtain went up and the lights dimmed, I looked across and Hope was just beaming from ear to ear, totally entranced by the whole thing. She was a little bit shy to begin with, but by the end of the show, she was jumping up and down, waving and shouting out the answers that the cast were asking. I ended up having to buy her chocolate, sweets, ice cream, a teddy and a balloon, but it was worth every penny, to see her so happy and proud of herself. Can't wait to take her again. She's grown up so much, even since going to the cinema.

Chapter Twenty Six - Happy Campers

I love how the kids have quirky obsessions and try to indulge them, as much as possible. Their current one is the TV Programme 'Friday Night Dinner.' It's such a good series. The two sons have moved out, but because they're Jewish, they come home every Friday night for their dinner and something always go wrong. It's one of those programmes, which we all love, even though the language can sometimes be a bit strong, it's just so good.

The kids decided that even though we're not Jewish, they wanted us to have Friday night dinners too. We all sit around the table and have our meal, followed by crumble. My kids don't eat anything that's slightly saucy, but because the family have it in the programme, it was a sacrifice my kids were willing to make and low and behold they found that they actually liked it. As far as I'm concerned this is a win-win. The children are happy, they try eating different foods and even better, they sit talking to us about their day, rather than looking down at their tablets or at the PC. The only downside came, when they decided they wanted traditional Jewish challah bread with their meal. After several long talks about how we're not Jewish, Jamie looked up specialist bakers on the internet and found a place (nine miles from our house) that makes and sells challah on Fridays. I told him that there was no way I was going to a proper bakers to buy Jewish bread.

At ten am on the next Friday, I was dutifully stood outside the bakers, waiting for my challah. I was so nervous, I thought they might take one look at me and refuse to sell me a loaf. Being the worrier that I am, I even researched on line, how to pronounce 'challah' properly. You kind of have to say it as if you have a hair in the back of your throat.

Luckily, the lady in the bakery was lovely and even complimented me on my pronunciation and we had the most beautiful, sweet, lovely challah bread with our meal and then all watched an episode of Friday Night Dinner together. It's the one time of the week, when meal time doesn't feel like a battle.

Once the dishes had been cleared away and loaded into the dishwasher, I managed to get ten minutes on the computer, while the kids happily watched a second episode of Friday Night Dinner. After searching for various online options. I booked a romantic night away in a hotel for our eighth wedding anniversary on Valentine's Day... at Legoland in Windsor. (Well we couldn't go anywhere without the kids could we ?)

At half past one in the morning, Jamie woke me up and said that he had a 'red throat.' Usually he gives you a warning that he has a 'purple throat' and then red is the most painful stage for him, but this one came out of nowhere. It was such fun playing 'hunt the Calpol' in the middle of the night!

At three o'clock I finally managed to get him to calm down and back off to sleep. I crept thankfully into my own bed and snuggled down underneath the warm covers. Exactly forty five minutes later, Hope came into our room and then kept fidgeting whilst she tried to get back to sleep, which meant that I couldn't nod off, because she kept nudging me awake again. Fifteen minutes after Hope had stumbled into the room, John's alarm went off, screaming that it was four o'clock, which fully woke Hope. Hearing her dad getting up and dressed, unsettled Hope even further and it took me until half past five to get her to go back to sleep. Once more, I gratefully sank underneath the duvet. Fifty minutes later, at twenty past six the alarm went off, because John had forgotten that it was the weekend and accidentally set the alarm for my usual get up time. I didn't even have the energy to cry.

To add insult to tired injury, Jamie's just developed a really annoying habit of walking laps around my bedroom, when he's annoyed that I haven't woken up early enough. It's sooo annoying and after the night I'd just had, I really didn't need it.

One more thing I didn't need, was Jamie's invite to an early morning, joint birthday party, which he was really excited about. It was held at a sports centre near his school and I was surprised that he wanted to go really. I took Hope with me and we went and had a drink, sitting in the café that helpfully overlooked the party area. We had a nice little time, whilst Hope played on her tablet and I watched her, yet was still on the alert for Jamie and any signs of an impending meltdown, meaning I might possibly have to spring into action to comfort him, at a moment's notice. Thankfully, he appeared to be coping well, whenever I looked up, but I couldn't believe it when I saw him thundering past in a race and he wasn't at the back.

When the activities were over, he rather rudely turned his nose up at the icing on the birthday cake and so we said our goodbyes and quickly left.

As we were driving home, we started talking about birthdays and what we would like for presents. My son, started to list all the things he wanted and I started to wonder about the likelihood of me winning the lottery, to pay for it all. To distract him, before he could add further items to his mental list and maybe even inspire him to think of the thought behind gifts and not the actual money spent, I said. "You know, for my birthday, all I'd really like is a bunch of daffodils. They're my absolute favourite flower, with their cheery little heads." I thought this was really nice of me. I wanted to ensure that he didn't feel any pressure to find me something and that narrowing it down to something cheap would really help him, but as quick as you like, Jamie shot back. "Well you'd better hope the ones in the garden come up then. Didn't you ?" The cheek of it!!!!

As soon as we walked into the house, Hope asked, "Mummy can we can camp out in the garden tonight please ?" Sometimes I just don't have the energy to fight her, but, I was just as persistent as she was. There was no way that I was going to spend the night under canvas. Not only is it the wrong time of year, but to be honest, even if it was the warmest summer day, we still wouldn't camp out. Not after the last time we decided to put up the tent, which went something like this:-

9.00 am. Hope asked if we could camp out in the garden. Told her I would think about it.

10.00 am. Hope kept pushing about the camping, but I still didn't know what to do. It was an unseasonably warm, but on the other hand, I HATE CAMPING.

10.30 am. I am ashamed to say, I gave in to peer pressure.

12.00pm. Dropped Hope off at nursery and as I walked back out the door, I heard her telling her key worker "we're going camping today." It's going to be a bit embarrassing at home time, if the staff ask us where we're going camping and I have to say 'the garden.'

3.20pm. Picked Jamie up from school and the first thing Hope told him, was about the camping.

4.00pm. The kids were deliriously excited about the camping. They put all their stuff ready in a pile, as soon as they got home.

5.00pm. John and I persuaded the kids to stay indoors, whilst we went to set the tent up.

5.05pm. Started feeling excited about the whole camping thing.

5.07pm. Told the kids to go back in and watch the TV, while we concentrated on the tent erecting.

5.10pm. John accidentally snapped one of the tent poles and then snapped at me, when I asked whether we could do without one tiny pole.

5.15pm. John stopped swearing about the tent pole and apologised.

5.17pm. Told the children that 'no they couldn't help and we would be a lot quicker if they went back in and watched TV.'

5.40pm. John got back from the camping shop with a pole replacement.

6.00pm. The tent was finally up and ready for inspection by the kids.

9.30pm. John took the kids on out in their pyjamas and cooked them sausages on the portable gas cooker (they had been cooking in the oven for at least twenty minutes beforehand. Not that the kids realised, but I didn't want to add food poisoning to the hypothermia we would all surely be suffering from, by tomorrow.)

9.45pm. Took out mugs of hot chocolates for them. Remembering just in time, to call them 'warm chocolates' because otherwise, Hope wouldn't drink hers.

9.55pm. Was just about ready to settle into my sleeping bag and trying desperately not to imagine rats gnawing their way through the flimsy tent material to get at us, when Hope insisted on a bed time story.

10.10pm. Read the story as quickly as possible and finally got everyone settled down and into their sleeping bags.

10.20pm. Was just getting comfortable, when Hope started crying, pleading to go back into the house.

10.25pm. Jamie said he was too cold and wanted to go in as well.

10.30pm. All tucked up in our bed, watching TV in the warm. So much for camping.

So there was absolutely no way, we were going camping. EVER!

John came home from work, to a roast dinner and two hyperactive children waiting for him. As soon as the food had been eaten, we piled into the car and went for a drive. We were going to 'surprise' the kids with a nice leisurely, healthy walk around the park, but when we got there, the kids refused to get out of the car.

As we made our way home again, with John in a foul mood at the petrol we had just wasted, I started singing along to Nickelback's song 'Rockstar' as it played on the radio. The second it had finished, Jamie said. "That song makes no sense." Now, I might not always know where his mind is going, but I do know that when he makes one of these pronouncements, my son is usually, always right. "Why does he sing about being skinny and not wanting to eat, but then in another part of the song he says that he doesn't want to pay for his meals and wants them given to him for free ?" I couldn't come up with a sufficient answer, on the basis that I wasn't there when they wrote the song, but Jamie was undeterred and went on for at least three hours, moaning about how it was a complete contradiction.

There was absolutely nothing I could say to stop him going on about it. It's like the Bletchley Circle all over again. It drives him crazy that the group of women in the programme are collectively called a 'circle,' but there are four of them and he's adamant that they should be named the Bletchley Square and he gets quite passionate about it, whenever it's on TV.

When we got home, the kids starting playing their recent favourite game. I don't get it. We have IKEA chairs and a conservatory full of toys, but for two days straight Hope has been sat watching TV in a washing basket and getting Jamie to pull her around in it, like it's a car. I can't explain it, but at least they're physically playing together. Until they discovered the delights of the wash basket, the only time they played together was whenever they decided to link up via a game on the internet and then it usually descends into tears, when they start trying to kill the other person's avatar.

As Jamie got tired from pulling such a heavy weight around, he went back to playing on the PC, while his sister happily watched a DVD on the little TV, from the confines of her basket.

Chapter Twenty Seven - Bearer of Bad Tidings

Today was the day of the school's Christmas Market. It used to be called the Christmas Fayre, but now it's been upgraded to 'market' to make people think it's going to be trendy and maybe even a little European, like those lovely German Christmas Markets that have sprung up everywhere in the last few years, in their little wooden huts. The reality is actually, trestle tables set around a huge hall that smells of feet. The tables are festooned with donated jars and tins of rubbish that no one wants, which now have a raffle ticket slapped on the front and are being passed off as something you would actually want to pay money to win. Next to these 'prizes' are cakes that have been made by parents, at homes with no hygiene certificates and have been stored all day in unknown circumstances and are covered by the hands of little people (who don't really have the best record in washing their hands after they've been to the toilet or picked their noses) and are now handling the cakes and putting back the ones they don't like.

Alongside the culinary delights, were very cheap sweets that were attracting so many children, they were twenty deep and the harassed, retired lady who had volunteered to man the stall, was looking as if she would gladly swap the entire stall contents for a bottle of vodka and a lie down.

Jamie gave a cursory glance to the stalls with broken toys and nineteen seventies jigsaws with missing pieces that no one wanted. There were dolls with missing arms and grubby looking plastic diggers and board games that had parts missing.

Every year, Jamie expects it to be good and every year he is disappointed and says he doesn't want to go again. Then, as Christmas rolls around once more, the school do some sort of hypnotism thing and persuade the kids into making us walk around in the room that smells of feet and stale sweat, spending money on trash. The one thing that the kids do like is, seeing Santa, so we made our way up to the smaller hall, which housed the hallowed grotto.

As parents, we knew that the old gentleman, Albert Phillips who had been standing in as Father Christmas for the last twenty years, had sadly passed away earlier in the year. Several of the parents had gone to pay their respects at the funeral of the lovely man who had been a part of our kid's lives every year. As a lovely gesture, his son Scott had agreed to pick up the mantle and volunteered to take his father's place as Santa.

As the children all stood in a queue, excitedly waiting for their opportunity to tell Father Christmas what they wanted to find under their Christmas tree on the big day, one of the school governor's cleared his throat, to make a speech.

Len Sweethead was a decrepit and universally loathed man, who seemed to have walked straight out of a Dicken's novel and all eyes swivelled in his direction, to see what he would say. No doubt, he was going to praise the work of the PTA in making the 'market' happen. The kids just wanted to see Santa, the last thing they wanted was a lecture. "Now, as some of you will know" Sweethead began "Father Christmas died a few months ago." I think he went on to say, that Santa had been replaced by his son, but his words had been drowned out by the mass hysteria he had unleashed. Kids were screaming, parents were shouting and Len Sweethead was trying to work out, why no one was appreciating his speech.

As a convoy, marched off in search of the headmistress, Jamie turned to me and said "Mummy, can we just go home please. I need time to come to terms with this rather sad news."

Chapter Twenty Eight - He's Gonna Find Out Who's Naughty Or Nice

Today we travelled to Legoland for a Santa Sleepover. We decided to go to Windsor Castle first and then into Windsor for Christmas shopping. When we got to the castle, Hope totally freaked out. She refused to go in and kept trying to run off up through the main street. "What's wrong Hope ?" I asked, dropping to my knees. I loosely held her arms and managed to get her to calm down enough, so that she would at least look at me. "I'm scared. I don't want to see the Queen." Trying not to laugh too hard and hurt her sensitive feelings, I assured her that her majesty wouldn't be home and even if she was, we wouldn't see her. This mollified her somewhat and we managed to carry on with our tour of the castle. It is such a beautiful building with so much history, yet all my two wanted to look at, were the many castle shops. As we left, Jamie carried a teddy that was dressed as a King (and cost a King's ransom) and Hope was furiously cuddling a plush Corgi that wore a tiara and a purple, ermine lined cape. After a quick bite to eat, at the first fast food restaurant we could find, we took on the high street shops.

There was a definite crispness to the air, the streets were festooned with Christmas lights and the children were excited about their Santa sleepover. Loaded down with shopping bags, we made our way back to the hotel.

The Legoland Hotel is Hope's favourite place ever and both the children were soon running around the room on a treasure hunt, which ended with them finding a bag of Lego each, in the treasure chest in our room. Waiting for us on the desk was a small wicker basket, which held a mince pie and a carrot. These weren't for eating however, there were instructions, stating that we had to leave the little basket outside the door when we went to bed and during the night, the elves would exchange them for the first clue needed in tomorrow's mass treasure hunt.

Once we had unpacked and the children had calmed down (but were still hyper by anyone else's standards) we had dinner in the hotel's themed restaurant. It's perfect for them, because it's an all you can eat buffet style restaurant. No one minds that your children can't sit still for more than two minutes at a time and hovering around the food, or constantly getting up to walk around, is expected.

We chose the package, because there is so much entertainment for the kids. There's discos and a meet and greet with a Lego Santa, as well as a pantomime, but Hope and Jamie totally refused to watch any of it. So by seven thirty we were all tucked up in bed watching TV.

Once they had finally fallen asleep, I opened the heavy door and looked along the corridor, every single door had a wicker basket outside it, containing a carrot and a mince pie. It was such a lovely sight, it made me feel all warm and fuzzy.

At five in the morning, I was rudely awaken by two excitable children jumping up and down on the bed with a piece of paper in their hands. Apparently the elves had popped the first clue under the door, ridiculously early. Hope looked like she was on an invisible pogo stick and neither of them would stop pestering us until we got dressed and ready to go downstairs.

We managed to convince (threaten) them into having breakfast first and then the treasure hunt began in earnest. It was quite a sight to behold, with leagues of children and reluctant parents scouring the halls for clues. When we had finished and the children had their rewards, it was time to head to the park itself, to meet Father Christmas.

We had paid quite a lot of money to see the bearded wonder, but the look on my face must have been priceless, as I watched Hope and Jamie totally clam up and refuse to even look at Santa. I did what I usually do in these situations, I over talk. Luckily Santa was OK with that and I just carried on answering for the children, like some sort of bizarre ventriloquist act.

It was all worth it however, when the kids were presented with their big red bags full of Lego goodies and they came away from the whole experience, whipped up into a festive frenzy.

Chapter Twenty Nine - The Littlest Showgirl In Town

The following day after our return from Windsor, I received an email from my Burlesque instructor saying that our hard work was paying off. We had picked up the routine so well that she wanted to know if we would agree to take part in the dance school's Christmas Show and inviting everyone to a meeting that very night, to discuss it. I couldn't wait.

At lunchtime, I was sat on the toilet, having a wee (like you do,) with the bathroom door open (like I do, because otherwise, the kids would dismantle it, in their efforts to be included in whatever I was doing.) John was in our bedroom, getting changed out of his work clothes. Jamie was at school and Hope was taking full advantage of the fact that her brother wasn't around to stop her and had gone into his room to look for one of his beloved comics. I looked up, to see Hope walk past me, engrossed in a comic she had found.

My brain didn't work fast enough to get the word 'stop' out, when I realised that she wasn't watching where she was going. Everything went into slow motion and I watched helpless, as she walked right off of the top step and cartwheeled down to the very bottom. The only noise, as she hit the floor, was me screaming. When you see someone fall like that on

TV, they generally don't get back up again. I was beyond hysterical. John managed to get to her first and she sat bolt upright and said "can I have a Kinder egg now please ?" It was literally the worst day of my life. Every time I closed my eyes, I could see her falling, it was horrendous. Evidently though, it was worse for me than it was for her.

Hours later, safe in the knowledge that Hope wasn't suffering any after effects and she hadn't hurt her head, I allowed John to force me out of the house and off to dance class.

I grabbed myself a coffee and sat down in the circle, excited and nervous at the prospect of the meeting and taking part in an actual performance. Apparently, the dance school give the students chance to perform throughout the year and they sell tickets to friends and family, so you can perform in a safe and nurturing atmosphere. Guests can buy soft and alcoholic drinks too, so it's a win for everyone. It does sound a bit like one big class assembly though, except this time, my proud husband will come and watch instead of my parents.

There was a nervous ripple of excitement, flying around the room as Fifi swayed into the room and started to discuss the routine. This was going to be the real deal, we had to go down to pasties, no one would be able to wear a baggy t-shirt over the top to preserve their modesty. After several minutes of looking nervously at one another, we all agreed. We were going to do this. Practising the routine suddenly felt different. There was a real desire to get this right and the pressure made people make silly mistakes, but overall it worked well. It still all seemed a bit unreal and I could tell that some of the other girls were wondering if they were doing the right thing, but Fifi Firecracker assured us that she wouldn't let us perform, if she didn't think we were ready for it. When I left class, I was fantasising about myself in a fifties film, dancing with Gene Kelly. I think delusions of grandeur really might be a bit of a problem for me.

When I got home, the kids were chattering excitedly about Christmas. The only bit of Christmas I really don't like is the time when friends come to the house with presents for the kids.

Don't get me wrong, I know it's really good of them to put their time and money into getting my children a gift, but it does pave the way for huge amounts of awkwardness. No matter how much I try and prepare the kids beforehand ("if you don't like something, just say thank you and tell Mummy about it later") and give them very clear instructions on how to handle it. When someone gives them something that they don't like, everything they'd previously agreed to do, goes flying out of the window, along with my pride. It is truly excruciating. I try to apologise for them and put it down to the Asperger's, but secretly, I think that it might actually be my fault.

When I was little, my Nan used to bring me sweets every week, one day she brought me a pair of white knee high socks instead. When she gave them to me, I promptly ran and chucked them in the bin. I can still clearly remember being told off by my Mum and told to apologise, which I resolutely refused to do. As far as I was concerned, it was my witless grandmother that needed to apologise. I mean who buys socks as a present ?

I still, as a thirty eight year old woman, find it difficult to hide my contempt for a rubbish present. I do this unconvincing, "thank you," but ten minutes later, I can't stop myself from asking "why on earth did you think I would like this ?" So perhaps I should stop blaming the kid's Asperger's and start looking a little closer to home.

Chapter Thirty - Santa Claus Is Coming To Town

Luckily (or unluckily) there had been a flu epidemic flying around the school and I had managed to put my friends off from delivering any presents in case they caught the bug. The days leading up to Christmas passed by in a blur of food, drink and TV programmes and suddenly it was Christmas morning!!!!!!!!!!!!!!!!!!!! I had been practising every other day for the Burlesque performance and I was looking forward to some peace and relaxation with my family.

I barely slept and for once it wasn't down to the kids. I kept thinking of all the presents waiting under the Christmas tree and getting myself over-excited. The kids were sound asleep, whilst I was the one lying in bed, listening out for sleigh bells or the sound of reindeer hooves on the roof.

At quarter to seven, I couldn't stand it any longer and I went down stairs, turned on the fairy lights and the fire and ran back upstairs shouting "he's been." The kids emerged blurry eyed from their bedrooms and I kept bouncing up and down, trying to hurry them along. "Come on, hurry up. Santa's been." Jamie fixed me with a stare and said "I'm not going anywhere, until I've cleaned my teeth. So please calm down. It's far too early."

I swear, it was the longest teeth cleaning session of my life, despite the fact that he put his little timer on and it was only two minutes, it felt like time had actually slowed down. As soon, as they both had sparkling pearly whites, they deigned to come downstairs and see their presents.

Each of them had a sofa filled with toys and if I had seen that as a kid, I would have been, thrilled and dived in, all you would have seen was a flurry of paper as I powered through. My kids however, are different to me. They carefully unwrapped each present and instead of saying "oh that's brilliant," they just looked at the toy and then told me the store that Santa must have got it from. It was somewhat of an anti-climax I can tell you.

The turkey was cooked, along with a joint of gammon, because Jamie said he doesn't like turkey, (despite having eaten it every year previously.) As usual, I served up mountains of food and the kids sat there, playing with it and hardly ate a bite. Jamie became very curious over my glass of champagne and so I said to him "would you like a sip?" He eyed me with concern, as if he were trying to decide whether to call the police on me and finally thought better of it "OK" he said and took a sip. Seconds later those expensive little bubbles were spat across my festive tablecloth, as Jamie declared. "Eugh that tasted like molten salt. I really can't believe you drink that stuff."

As soon as they got down from the table, professing that they weren't hungry, I knew it would be a maximum of ten minutes before they started on the Christmas chocolate and sweets, but I wasn't going to stand in their way, Christmas wouldn't be Christmas without a monumental sugar rush.

Darkness descended and the wine flowed, Christmas Day had once more come to an end and the children happily fell asleep surrounded by piles of toys. They had gone from excitement to euphoria, through to screaming that they weren't tired or hyped up on sugar, until back to excitement again, before crashing out altogether. John and I lay in bed underneath the covers, eating chocolates and drinking wine, as we watched a Christmas comedy special and congratulated ourselves on another wonderful Christmas day.

I can honestly say, Christmas was like having a baby. Weeks of anxiety and excitement leading up to the big day. Lots of planning and expectation and expensive items needing to be bought. Then it arrives and you have the family round bringing presents, the house is so full of stuff that you don't know where you're going to fit it all, you're eating and sleeping at odd hours and it feels like your life will never get back into a routine again. However, by the time, the next one comes along, you've forgotten the pain of the last one and you can't wait to do it all over again.

Chapter Thirty One - A New Year

New Year's Eve was the night of the big performance. I got there early in the afternoon and helped some of the girls to set out the bottles of beer, lemonade and wine for the makeshift bar and the rows of plastic school chairs. There was a really great atmosphere and everyone was excited and nervous, so no one felt like they were alone with their own thoughts. We had practised until we could do the routine in our sleep (and on a couple of nights, I think I might actually have done that.) It was too late to back out. The show would go on.

Once everything was ready and everyone was happy with the hard work we'd all put in, it was time for a full dress rehearsal. Only when we were standing on the actual stage, after weeks of practice, did it dawn on us that the next time we would perform this, there would be an actual audience, with camera phones, watching our every move.

Downstairs, was a vast white room, with floor to ceiling mirrors, which we all sat around, helping each other to apply fake tan, fastening corsets, straightening stocking seams and ensuring pasties were properly affixed. Make up was carefully applied and then, when we were all looking showgirl perfect, we got out the hip flasks and bottles of vodka (for courage obviously,) drinking spirits out of little plastic cups, we'd pinched from the water cooler.

One by one, the different acts would disappear upstairs and five minutes later, come back down all exhilarated and happy, but for the ones left waiting, the anticipation was agony. Finally, we were called and that walk up the fifteen stepped staircase seemed to take a lifetime. We had to wait for the act in front to finish and the music seemed to go on forever, then all at once, time seemed to speed up and it was our turn to go on.

I caught sight of John sitting in the third row (the kids were at home with my Dad and Step-Mum) and I strutted out onto the stage, wearing black patent stilettos, seamed stockings, a black vintage suspender belt over black frilly knickers and a deep red, boned corset (with red sequined tasselled pasties underneath,) elbow length black satin gloves and a small black top hat with a little lace veil on top, set at a jaunty angle, completed the outfit. I looked the part, but my insides were quaking as I plastered on a fake smile and took my pose, ready for the music to start.

Performing was a bit like having an out of body experience and I know I made a few minor mistakes, but time went by so fast and I can't really remember the performance, but what was clearly imprinted on my memory, was the roar of the crowd, when we turned around and threw our corsets away, revealing our pasties, with all our tassels swinging in the air.

I know that a lot of people don't agree with this sort of thing and think the women are being exploited and they are obviously entitled to hold that opinion.

However, for me the rush of adrenaline and the thrill of it all, as I cast aside my corset, gave me a feeling of immense empowerment. We all ran downstairs in an excited group, hugging one another in joy and chattering madly about what went well and what bits didn't go so well.

I know now, that even if I'm scared, I can overcome anything. Plus, I was now filled with the desire to go and rip my clothes off on stage again, perhaps even in a solo performance.

John seemed very pleased to be going home with a stripper and kept telling me how proud he was, he even held the car door open for me and he hasn't done that since we first started dating.

I sat on the sofa, recounting the night to my supportive family, before I took the kids up to bed. My Dad and Step-Mum left to go home, to see to their dogs before the bangs of the fireworks started and Hope fell instantly asleep in my arms. Jamie however, was determined to stay awake until midnight and see the New Year in, for the first time ever.

Bless him, poor Jamie made it all the way until five minutes to midnight. No matter, how I tried to wake him, it was no use. He slept right through the fireworks without stirring and all I could do, was to carry him to his own bed to continue sleeping.

At three in the morning, I felt the bed shaking and woke to find a stressed out son standing over me. "I've had an accident, Mummy" he said.

Groaning and shaking a little, through lack of sleep, I washed him down, helped him dry himself off and found him a new pair of boxer shirts. Luckily, he had managed to get to the bathroom, but unfortunately, he hadn't managed to aim into the toilet properly and had somehow urinated all down his legs.

As we went into his room, and sat on his warm cosy bed, his curtains were wide open, allowing some natural light into the room, so it wasn't so dark. There were no clouds and the sky was an immense blanket of darkness, studded with sparkling silver stars. Jamie was wide awake after the impromptu cleaning and changing. Wordlessly, he sat on his bed, leaning on the windowsill, gazing in wonder at the night sky.

Despite being utterly exhausted, I put my arm around his shoulders and we sat there, just the two of us, pointing out the different constellations, until his eyelids began to droop and he became sleepy.

I sat at the end of his bed and watched my little boy as he finally drifted off to sleep and thanked those same heavenly stars, that I had such special children

I was feeling far more positive about the New Year that had just begun. I had conquered my fears and come through the other side, happier and stronger. There would be no stopping me now.

All I have to keep in mind is, that even if I'm sleep deprived, you should always remember to take some time, to just sit and look at the stars at three in the morning.

A Bit About My Aspies

When my son was born, my only experience of Autism, was of watching the film 'Rain Man.' As he grew, we had no concerns about him at all. He was an only child and I had no friends who had children and so I had nothing to compare him against. I guess, I had subconsciously fitted everything around him and did everything the way he liked, so we never had any issues. As an only child, he was in a loving, stable and calm household, where he was the centre of our universe and everything was orderly.

It was only when my beautiful boy went to the nursery section of a private school that problems started to occur. In the unpredictable atmosphere of the nursery, traits were starting to show themselves. We got called in for a meeting with the Headmistress and his Key Worker and they said that he wouldn't be able to carry on at the school and would have to leave at the end of the academic year. They said they thought it was possibly Autism and that we should go and speak to our family GP.

We went to the GP and because we had no concerns, our Doctor put it down to the rigidity of the school and a precocious little boy, who had no experience of being around other children.

The end of the school year was truly devastating. He loved his Key Worker and I remember standing in the doorway on the last day and all his little friends saying to her "bye Miss, see you next year" and I knew that my little boy was being cast out. It was even more humiliating than when they had banned him from taking part in the nursery nativity at Christmas. Mothers with eyes welling up and wobbly chins, were showing their photos around of their little ones and I had to stand there, embarrassed and saddened.

We found him a lovely little rural school, set amongst quiet farmland in a village about twelve miles away from our house. His nursery had told us far too late, that he wouldn't be able to continue and we didn't have much in the way of options for reception class places. We went along for a familiarisation day and whilst the children were in the classroom with their new friends, us adults, were sent to have tea or coffee in the hall. At the end of the day, we stepped outside into the playground and we could see our son's classroom door was open. There were a couple of parents already stood there talking to the teacher and we watched open mouthed, as we saw our son, walk out of the classroom unobserved. We followed him to the gate, which parents coming the other way, helpfully held open for him and then followed him down on to the main road, where he had gone to look for our car.

Naturally, we complained about this to the Headmistress the next day and her response was "well it's all about boundaries really. If he's going to run away, he's going to run away and there's not much we can do about it." That was the last time that he ever went to that school.

We had even less choice, by this point, when it came to finding a school place. As luck would have it, we found a space in a school, in the next city to ours and went along for their familiarisation day. I think we were there for all of five minutes, when the Headmistress looked at us and said "you know he's on the spectrum don't you ?" I knew in that instant that we couldn't deny it anymore. We went back to the GP and got him a referral. It was a hard two years and we saw a lot of Paediatricians in that time, some that wanted to simply medicate him and others that told us "labelling a child won't help anyone." Eventually, we got our diagnosis and breathed a huge sigh of relief.

When he was five, he had a boost of hormones around the same time that his sister was born and I've got to admit, things were quite tough at first, but going on the National Autistic Society's Earlybird Plus course, really helped to validate everything that we had been doing for him anyway. I used to be scared about what the future held for him, but I'm not so worried anymore. He is growing up to be a very articulate and intelligent young man. Obviously he gets his off days (don't we all ?) He still has areas to improve in (don't we all ?) He is exceeding our expectations, every day.

When our daughter was born, she was a delight. She was such a placid, beautiful, smiley little girl and at the age of one years old, we declared that she definitely didn't have Asperger's. When she was around two however, I started getting my doubts.

People tried to talk me out of it and said that perhaps she was picking up cues from her brother, but I knew it wasn't that. She was showing behaviours that, my son had only exhibited, before she was born. The things that concerned me were, her shyness. She wouldn't talk in front of other people, she screamed if she saw anyone with dark hair (and I mean really scream and get upset,) she put her hands over her ears if there was a loud noise and if I failed to interpret her demands, she would have a meltdown and hide under a table.

Whilst I was on the Earlybird Plus course for our son, I voiced my opinions about my little girl to the tutor and she suggested that I should maybe pop along and ask our GP what he thought. Family members thought I was wrong, indeed I doubted myself, but a week later I found myself seated in front of a Doctor, with my daughter hiding behind me, taking pictures of the doctor through her DS camera. I made my case, whilst wondering whether I would be laughed out of the room, but a referral was made. Things had been reformed in Autism services in our city, since our son had been diagnosed. I took my little girl to see a Paediatrician and she spent the whole appointment, curled into a ball, not looking at the dark haired professional.

Next we were sent to see a Doctor and Speech Therapist (at the same time,) the Doctor observed and also asked me questions, whilst the Therapist tried to engage my daughter in balloons and moving toys. At the end of the hour, my three year old, had a diagnosis of Asperger's Syndrome and Pathological Demand Avoidance! Without a two year fight!

My little girl is thrilled that she has the same thing as her brother and although I was worried, she started school two months ago and is doing amazingly well. I am so thankful to have my two. I didn't realise I had such reserves of love, compassion and patience until I had them.

What are the Signs ?

The questions that I get asked the most are "what is Asperger's ?" or "what are the signs, as I think my child/my nephew has it ?"

When I took my daughter along to the Doctor, I just wanted someone to look at her and say "yes I think you may have grounds for concern" or "don't be silly, she's fine." Be prepared for a long wait to see a specialist, but if you are concerned, then its worth going along. You have no idea how many times I have talked myself out of it. It's hard, but at the end of the day, staying in denial doesn't help your child, if they are going to need support, help and understanding.

I have compiled a list of some of the most common symptoms for Asperger's Syndrome, Pathological Demand Avoidance Syndrome and Autistic Spectrum Disorder. Children may have just one of these, and not display all of the symptoms, but if you have any concerns, have a look, research it more online if needed and if you're still concerned, make an appointment with your GP.

If you have doubts, go with your own instinct and don't allow others to talk you out of it, until you've consulted a medical professional.

Asperger's Syndrome

- Lack of empathy with others
- Very rigid thinking
- Difficulty controlling emotions
- Limited and obsessive interests
- Ritualistic behaviour
- Difficulty with imaginative and creative play
- Impaired motor skills
- Sensory problems
- Difficulty interacting with others
- Communication difficulties
- Difficulty in waiting or taking turns
- Odd or repetitive movements

Autistic Spectrum Disorder

- Difficulties with non-verbal communication
- Problems developing peer group friendships
- Verbal communication delay
- Repetitive use of language
- Rocking or flapping movements
- Lack of empathy with others
- Problems initiating conversations
- Sensory problems

Pathological Demand Avoidance Syndrome

- Socially manipulative

- An anxiety controlled inability to comply with demands
- Good use of eye contact
- Usually placid in their first twelve months
- Problems with verbal development
- Overwhelming need to control situations and people
- Skilled use of distraction techniques when asked a question

Things that I wish someone had explained to me about Asperger's and Autism

- On a stress level of 1-10 (1 being the lowest,) most people wake up on a level 2 and their stress level may increase to a 6 or 7 throughout the day. Children on the spectrum, are more likely to wake up, already at level 7. The demands of brushing their teeth, having to wash, eat breakfast and get dressed, can send them way past 10, before they even step outside the door. It was only when this was explained, that I realised why my son was waking up angry and made sure I kept calm and made allowances for him.

- I used to say to my son, "pick your shoes up" or whatever I wanted him to do and he wouldn't acknowledge my request. I would usually end up shouting and then so would he and the socks would remain on the floor, whilst we had an argument. I learnt that, he sometimes ignored me, because he was totally absorbed in whatever he was doing at the time, but more often than not, it was because he didn't realise I was talking to him.

He even said this to me once, when we were the only two people in the house and I was shouting at him for not answering me. It just didn't occur to him, that I was addressing him. To save time and stress, I always make sure that I say his name and make sure that I have his full attention, before I begin talking to him. It's a small thing, but it's effective.

- If you're trying to explain something to your child and they're not understanding what you're trying to say. Get a piece of paper and draw what you want to say. You don't need to be an artist to do it. Children on the spectrum respond better to visuals than abstract thoughts.

- Even if your child has Asperger's and is quite verbal, you will still need to stand up for them on occasion. I don't like to use the term 'fight for' because it's sounds a bit aggressive, but be prepared, that your child is vulnerable in certain areas and they are unable to properly make their feelings felt or to make sure they are getting a fair deal. Similarly, be prepared for people to think of you as too overbearing or over protective, because all they'll see is you on your soap box all the time. Just remember, that as long as you're respectful, don't worry about other people's opinions. Put your child first and grow a thicker skin.

- When giving instructions or imparting information to your child, try to use the least amount of words possible, as too much vocabulary, could confuse and upset them.

- In order to get support for your child at school, you may need to fill in supporting paperwork, giving evidence of the behaviours your child exhibits. I found this really upsetting the first time I had to do it. It felt like a massive betrayal, pointing out all the faults of my perfect son. Detach yourself from the emotional side of it and be prepared to write out the worst case scenario. It has to be done, in order to get them help. Similarly, the school will have to do this and any other supporting professionals. It's easy to get despondent when you see everything negative about your child written in black and white, but remember, this is in your child's best interest and is there to highlight the darkest side, not the most positive. If everything was portrayed as wonderful, there wouldn't be any help offered.

Helpful Organisations

The National Autistic Society, 393 City Road, London
EC1V 1NG. NAS Helpline: 0845 070 4004.

NAS Earlybird Centre, Barnsley Road, Dodworth,
Barnsley S75 3JT. Tel: 01226 779218.

Disability Benefit Enquiry Line: 0800 882200.

IPSEA: Independent Panel for Special Education
Advice. Advice Line: 0800 0184016.

PDA Society: info@pdasociety.org.uk

Further Useful Reading

<u>Non-Fiction</u>

Aspergirls by Rudy Simone
Understanding Pathological Demand Avoidance
Syndrome in Children by Phil Christie, Margaret
Duncan, Ruth Fidler and Zara Healy
Freaks, Geeks and Asperger's Syndrome by Luke
Jackson
The reason I jump by Naoki Higashida
Asperger's Syndrome for Dummies by Gina Gomez de
la Cuesta and James Mason
The Complete Guide to Asperger's Syndrome by Tony
Attwood

<u>Fiction</u>

The Curious Incident of the Dog in the Night Time by
Mark Haddon
Rubbernecker by Belinda Bauer

Fiction Aimed At Children

Dude I'm an Aspie by Matt Friedman
When my worries get too big by Kari Dunn Buron

About the Author

Sarah Sprules lives in the South West of England with her husband and two children, who both have Asperger's Syndrome and Pathological Demand Avoidance. When not writing or running around after her children, Sarah can be found lecturing on how to self-publish novels, obsessing over Katy Perry or dreaming about the Isle of Wight.

For updates and to contact the author, you can find her on:

www.facebook.com/sarahsscriptorium, on Twitter @Sprulesy1, or email: sarahsscriptorium@fsmail.net

11783232R00106

Printed in Great Britain
by Amazon.co.uk, Ltd.,
Marston Gate.